Anger Strategies

Practical Tools For Professionals Treating Anger

This workbook consists of 7 sections with 42 modules for structured interventions, pertinent didactic, and reproducible handouts. A compact disc, Imageries, is included.

Claudia Black, Ph.D.

This workbook is one of a series of four tools for professionals.

Strategies Series:
Anger Strategies
Depression Strategies
Family Strategies
Relapse Toolkit Strategies

Copyright © 2006 by Claudia Black
Cover design by Martha Heier – PHX Productions
10 Digit ISBN 0-910223-30-0
13 Digit ISBN 978-0-910223-30-0
Mac Publishing
800.698.0148
claudiablack.com

Special thanks

To the talented and enthusiastic group that has become the team behind the books in the Strategies Series.

Sandi Klein, my assistant, who is invaluable as she skillfully works with every aspect of this project from writing, to organizing, editing, proofing, and coordinating the many parties involved...

Jeri Nilsen for her wonderful skills as editor...

To Martha Heier whose cover design and production work make this book a reality...

Jack Fahey, my husband and colleague, who is the sounding board for my creative process...

Together we have made a great team.

Note from Claudia Black

Anybody can become angry — that is easy, but to be angry with the right person and to the right degree and at the right time and for the right purpose, and in the right way — that is not within everybody's power and is not easy.

Aristotle, from *The Nicomachean Ethics*

Conflict, frustration and anger are all a part of the bargain of being alive. Anger is a natural human emotion. When we feel anger, our bodies and minds are telling us to pay attention and look at what is occurring around us. Anger energizes a person to act; to focus and identify what it is he or she is feeling or needing; and it helps to establish appropriate boundaries and limits. Anger needs space to be heard. When one listens to their anger instead of avoiding it or allowing it to mask other feelings or issues, it helps one to recognize choices as to whether or not to act, how to act, and then withdraw the investment in staying angry. Yet, anger is a frequently distorted and twisted emotion becoming a barrier to being present with one's self, and a significant barrier to healthy relationships. The goal is not to be afraid of anger, or to run from conflict, but to realize it gives us valuable information about others and ourselves.

It is my hope that this book will be a valuable aid to counselors, mental health practitioners and health care providers who are working with clients whose anger is causing difficulties in significant areas of their life. These difficulties may range from how they view and feel about themselves, to parenting skills, partner relationships, performance in the workplace, legal issues and overall health. With the foundation of good client assessment and intervention, Anger Strategies will be of great assistance in working with these clients.

Some clients may be participating in an anger management group as a consequence of domestic violence or other illegal behaviors that have arisen from their inappropriate expression of anger. Others may be in individual, couples, or family therapy and their anger becomes identified as a crucial clinical issue. Irrespective of the manner in which clients have come to you, their anger has become distorted and twisted and is conveyed in ways that create shame and blame. When anger becomes rage it hurts everyone involved and it can even kill. When it becomes internalized it is comparable to taking a dose of slow acting poison every day. While some clients are more motivated to change than others, the strategies in this book will assist in both motivation and change. To see there is a path moving away from the destruction of unhealthy anger, to develop a specific plan of action, and to know help is available allows clients to take the risks that will lead them to greater choices in how they live their lives.

If you are working with someone who despite previous anger-focused treatment has continued their anger behavior, it could be due to coexisting disorders that have not been adequately identified or treated. The most likely of these is addiction and depression. It is important to be aware of the association of addiction and anger and be willing to explore this possibility with clients. The assessment of substance abuse should be an integral part of any formal anger program. Any clinicians who do not feel qualified to make such an assessment should develop a relationship with a local provider. If a client is actively addicted, it is unlikely an anger treatment program or therapy will be effective until the addiction issues have been addressed. It is possible to address both at the same time, but the addiction needs to be the primary and priority issue.

It is also common for people with anger problems to be depressed. This may range from a diagnosis of bipolar to dysthymic or major depression. Other co-morbid issues may be anxiety disorders, possibly post-traumatic stress disorder, and frequently attention deficit disorders. Anger issues are also common to those with a history of brain injury or disease. If this is suspected for any of your clients, appropriate diagnosis and medications may be necessary to allow them to respond to treatment for anger issues. Again it is important to work in collaboration with other mental health and health care professionals.

In many of the Anger Strategies sections ideas and formats are presented for structured interventions, often including the use of handouts in the form of written exercises, checklists, sentence stems, structured dialogues, and/or art activities. All handouts are designed for clinicians to reproduce and use without restriction as to copyright permission.

The audio CD, Imageries, offers structured meditations for recovery. The disc contains four imageries: Relaxation Exercise, Inner Child Affirmation, Inner Source of Wisdom, and Letting Go and Receiving. It can be used in a group or individual setting.

Realizing I cannot consider all of the possible ethnic, cultural, and educational differences a clinician may be confronted with, I trust that sound clinical judgment will be used in the timing and use of these strategies. I encourage modifying them in any manner to tailor them to be more effective in helping clients stop their self-defeating behaviors and practice healthier relational skills.

Table of Contents

Section Six: Spiritual Strategies

Section Seven: Closing Strategies

Closing Thoughts

Outline of Anger Strategies

The outline is of a time-limited, structured psycho-educational therapy process with its focus on anger. While it is presented with a group orientation, it can also be used effectively with an individual. Read through all of the sessions and become familiar with the content so that you will be able to be flexible as needed. You know the needs of your clients better than the author. You may want to use all of the sessions in the sequence presented, or you may simply pick and choose those that are most relevant to your clients. Be creative and bring your own style of work into this process. Remember, this outline is meant only to be a guide.

Suggested Time

Time required for each session depends on whether or not this guide is used with an individual, or in a group setting. Sessions can be condensed or expanded by use of opening and closing rituals, time allotted to complete exercises, and depth of discussion. Know how much time you want to give the opening and closing rituals so that you will easily transition to the focus of the particular session. While most sessions for a group take one and one half hours, they could be expanded to a lengthier format, or condensed for an individual.

Suggested Opening of Each Session

Sessions are to begin and end on time with a ritual opening and closing of each session. The author suggests the sessions open with one or more of the following possibilities:

- A centering technique such as a relaxation exercise.
- A centering check in, where each participant shares with one or two words what they are experiencing physically (e.g.; tired, energetic), emotionally (e.g.; frustrated, lonely), and spiritually (e.g.; apart from, in tune with, at peace, disconnected).
- A review of the last session by the facilitator followed by each participant responding by identifying what they valued most from the previous session.
- A question or comment period about the previous session.
- Reading from a daily self-help meditation book.

Confidentiality

Consult your state regulations; the most common exceptions regard suicide, homicide, child and elder abuse. Explain your professional and/or agency's parameters of confidentiality at the time of initial meeting. Each session needs to begin with a statement of confidentiality. Suggested form: a pledge that each individual makes. "I pledge what I see, do, and hear here will stay here." The facilitator should expound that statement as required by state and federal regulations such as adding *except in the interest of your treatment with other treatment team members and in regard to state and federal regulations.*

1

Safety Issues

Should you have a client who is having difficulty containing his or her anger, or you perceive them to be at risk to others or themselves, he/she needs to be evaluated immediately for further assessment and appropriate referral. Facilitators are charged with protecting the physical safety of all of their clients, their families, and the general public.

The concept of time-out must be explained if you are working with any client whose anger is verbally and/or physically combative. A time-out is removing oneself from the setting before any verbal or physical altercation occurs. Time-out is a responsible action that prevents irresponsible actions. Constructive time-out entails more that just having a client walk away from a bad situation. There are many tactics a client could take during a time-out that will help him or her calm down. These include taking a walk, doing a relaxation exercise, attending a self-help meeting, or talking with someone who will help the client de-escalate. If a client is known to readily escalate into combative anger, facilitator may want to anticipate naming a specific person whom the client could reach out to. The purpose in engaging another person is not to discuss the details of the situation, but to aid the client to calm down, garner clarity about his or her thoughts and feelings, practice recovery skills, and/or problem solve revisiting the situation. Competitive sports, aggressive and sexually stimulating activities need to be avoided during a time-out as they reinforce the adrenaline rush the angry client is experiencing. Individuals who utilize a time-out must be committed to returning to the situation that triggered the anger after they have regained control, otherwise time-outs are employed as merely one more manipulative behavior to avoid the issue, evade problems, or wielded as a weapon against others.

A time-out can range from five minutes to a few hours and is taken so that a client can express him or herself without getting lost in personal attacks, defensiveness, and rage. Time-outs are utilized only after attempting to use other means of anger management. They are a last resort tactic meant to prevent a situation from escalating.

Didactic

Didactic refers to educational information that you may offer in a lecture type format. This is information you are welcome to use verbatim or as a model to improvise upon. When the session includes such information, it will be indicated with the word Didactic. To signify that the didactic portion has come to a close, this icon will be used.

 Didactic closed

When the didactic is resumed, the inverse of this icon will so indicate.

 Didactic resumed

Handouts

Handouts are included and part of most sessions. You may reproduce them without restriction as to copyright permission. Many of the handouts are best completed and discussed during the course of a particular session while others may be given as an assignment.

Assignments

Depending upon the motivation of clients and the session length, assignments most relevant to the focus on recovery are often an expedient use of their time. Prior to offering an assignment, garner their commitment to follow through. Be clear with instructions and expectations. Always follow up on the assignment in the subsequent session. When a client chooses not to do an assignment, consider the following:

1. Spend some time in the session working on an assignment that was unfinished.

2. Evaluate your initial rationale and explanation of the tasks; e.g., "Did I make the task(s) clear, simple, and linked to some payoff/benefit; or, did the participant perceive it as busy work?"

3. Evaluate the appropriate fit between the task assigned and the client's ability to perform it; e.g., is the unmet assignment related to participant's inability to perform it or unwillingness to comply? Could you facilitate the success by breaking assignments down into smaller more easily performable pieces?

4. Encourage client to observe, day-by-day, her/his skillful efforts to avoid, resist, and deceive self with reasons to fail. Make them expert observers of self-sabotage.

5. Examine precisely all decisions that the client makes during the interval between sessions to avoid follow through, and label them the client's "decisions," "choices."

Guided Imageries

A compact disc **Imageries** is included in this workbook. The disc contains four imageries: Relaxation Exercise, Inner Child Affirmation, Inner Source of Wisdom, and Letting Go and Receiving.

Suggested Closing of Each Session

Ask clients to respond to one of the following remarks:

- I learned that…
- I was surprised that…
- I remembered that…
- What I would like to learn more about is…
- What I did not understand was…

Asking the clients to make these statements further validates their participation and experience. It is also helpful for you to hear what they prioritize in terms of their learning experience.

Twelve Step Resources

Twelve Step programs are a valuable resource for participants with addiction problems. Due to the high association between addiction and anger, you are encouraged to be familiar with Twelve Step programs and their availability as a potential resource for your clients. Programs for substance abuse such as Alcoholics Anonymous (AA), Cocaine

INSTRUCTIONS

Anonymous (CA) or Narcotics Anonymous (NA) are found in most communities throughout the United States and throughout much of the world. Other Twelve Step groups such as Overeaters Anonymous (OA), Gamblers Anonymous (GA), or Sex Addicts Anonymous (SAA) are more limited in availability but may be very appropriate recommendations for specific clients.

Additional Tools

Claudia Black, the author, has created several videos, books, and audio CDs that closely correspond to various sessions. To order these directly, visit her website at www.claudiablack.com or call 1-800-698-0148.

Relevant titles are:

The Stamp Game: A Game of Feelings (for people of all ages)

Videos
Anger
Issues of Recovery
Double Jeopardy: Addiction and Depression
Relapse: The Illusion of Immunity
Relationship Series
Shame

Books
It Will Never Happen to Me: Growing Up With Addiction as Youngsters, Adolescents & Adults
Changing Course: Healing from Loss, Abandonment and Fear
A Hole in the Sidewalk: The Recovering Person's Guide to Relapse Prevention

Audio CDs
A Time for Healing from Abandonment and Shame
Putting the Past Behind: Steps in Recovery and Foundational Core Issues
Letting Go Imageries

Anger History Strategies

Overview of
Anger History Strategies

This section presents a variety of discussion formats for assisting clients in depicting a thorough representation of the role of anger in their lives. People with anger problems have seldom given thought to or talked directly about their anger; they have simply lived it. These sessions will assist in recognizing anger as a natural feeling that has a rightful place in one's emotional repertoire. For many people anger becomes distorted, inappropriately expressed and causes significant problems in their lives. With structured interventions clients will be able to talk about their anger, step away from it, view it, analyze their relationship with it, and recognize the motivation for their behavior. Consequently, they are helped to realize they have choices and the ability to relate to anger in a healthy manner.

Anger's Many Faces is a warm-up dialogue for clients to begin to recognize the many different ways anger is projected and then to talk about their anger. It will assist the facilitator to assess clients' self-awareness and insight into their behavior.

Expression and Roles of Anger is an important sequel to Anger's Many Faces. It will aid clients to recognize and be accountable for how they have used their anger.

Anger Line offers clients the opportunity to be more specific about anger incidents and behavior throughout their lives. The structure of this session will help in the recognition of anger patterns. Acknowledging that many people go to great lengths to avoid anger only to have it surface in distorted or hostile behaviors, the concept of anger avoidance is also introduced.

In the Red Zone facilitates clients owning their relationship to anger. It also begins the process of recognizing the multi-generational repetition of anger via the family system.

Anger Collage uses art therapy in the form of a collage to facilitate discussion of experiences often defended and not recognized in traditional talk therapy.

Family Gift boldly suggests that clients were the recipients of unjust anger in their growing up years and that they are repeating the behavior that was once modeled to them.

Anger's Many Faces

Objectives

To increase insight of negative or positive effects of anger.
To educate clients on the many ways anger may be expressed.

Materials Needed

Handout – Anger's Many Faces

Starting Point

The responses to the following questions can provide a wealth of information in a short period of time and is valuable as a warm-up dialogue to facilitate discussion. Clients can share their responses in a dyad (groups of two) or triad (groups of three), or as a large group. Pose the questions sequentially one at a time.

1. *Identify when you last became angry. What did you do with the anger?*
   Typically, not always, what they did the last time they became angry is what they commonly do when angry.

2. *How did that feel?*
   The response to "how did that feel?" provides a moral indicator regarding their beliefs about their behavior.

3. *Have you ever had problems as a result of your anger?* Explain.
   The response allows you to hear their perception of whether or not anger is problematic for them.

4. *Has your anger ever produced positive results?* Explain.
   Anger can be positive and the response to this question reveals whether or not they can make that association and also what they gauge to be "positive."

5. *What is your most memorable anger incident?* Explain.
   Their responses provide you with insight as to what they see to be of importance either negatively or positively.

Continue by presenting a description of the many faces of anger. Lead a discussion using the handout Anger's Many Faces as an outline; ask clients to offer examples as you describe the types of anger and add examples relevant to your clients.

Didactic

Anger is a normal, natural human emotion and your goal here is not to get rid of anger, but to take responsibility for how you express it. Anger does not have to lead to aggression or attack, nor does it have to hurt anyone. Expressed and tolerated appropriately, anger helps to create and maintain boundaries, it aids towards identifying your needs, and it is used as a form of self- protection.

Anger shows itself in many ways. On your handout check the boxes that indicate whether or not you identify with any of these portrayals of anger.

Passive-Aggressive
This is anger behavior, e.g. being late to a scheduled meeting be it with a family member, boss, or probation officer; you don't want to be there, or you feel you should be leading the meeting, but believing you can't avoid it, in irritation you are deliberately late. Or saying you will do something and then you don't do it, or taking forever to do it because you resent the obligation.

Caustic Remarks, Sarcasm
This is a comment muttered as you leave a meeting at work where you didn't feel your side was acknowledged; or after asking a spouse or partner to do something and it's not done to your satisfaction. It's the caustic remark muttered under your breath, "I should have done it myself if I wanted it done right."

Verbal Abuse
Verbal abuse can range from getting in someone's face and screaming, "Who told you . . . ?" "How could you . . . ?" "Why did you . . . ?" to name calling and telling someone they are worthless, etc.

Blaming
Blaming can range from not being accountable to accusing others as being "always at fault," e.g. wife, mother, boss, cop, neighbor, the bank — anyone but yourself.

Guerrilla Humor
Waging a verbal attack, or being insulting, and then calling it a joke and retreating behind a smile. Often followed by stating, "You're being too sensitive, I was just teasing."

Retaliatory Anger
Someone has said or done something to you that is hurtful and very upsetting and you seek a way to get revenge; for example, your husband or partner says something cruel and hurtful about you in front of his friends. You remain calm and just laugh it off, it's no big deal, but eventually you find a way to get even. Going on a spending binge that your husband or partner has to pay for or having an affair to make him feel bad are demonstrations of retaliating in anger.

Blind Rage
You are driving down the road, kids in the car, everything seems fine, and suddenly the driver in front of you cuts you off. You become furious and tailgate the guy, waving him over, flipping him the finger and are ready to fight on the side of the freeway if he pulled over; or the fellow at the bar, or the neighbor across the street gives you a wrong look. Or while watching TV your child or spouse/partner doesn't fetch a beer fast enough and you backhand them across the face. Blind rage often leads to violence. There is no middle ground.

Isolation
You stay away from people and take on the angry attitude that you don't like people and don't need them. This results in you leaving other people alone and in turn other people leave you alone.

Depression
Anger may be masked by depression. Depression is very complex and can encompass many issues. It could be purely biological — perhaps you are physiologically predisposed to depression. For many people it is about unresolved grief and sorrow. For some, depression is anger turned inward. It is the result of not being able to externalize anger (expressing it outwardly) and thereby keeping it all in — internalizing it.

The person who internalizes anger is often intensely frightened of rejection and abandonment should they show anger; or they equate anger with abuse. They believe that if they really get in touch with their anger they will become abusive; or if they show their anger others will become abusive towards them.

So it is no surprise when a depressed person expresses anger or hostility. They do it in the same ways others show anger, just more sporadically — in little bursts. They may be procrastinators, show sarcasm, or go into a fit of blind rage, physically assaulting someone. However, being a person who tends to take their feelings inward, they are probably more likely to assault themselves, as in acts of self-injury, self-mutilation, repetitive accidents, and the ultimate . . . suicide.

Have clients share the faces of anger they most identify with and ask them to give examples.

Anger's Many Faces

Identify and discuss your most common anger stances:

- ☐ Passive-aggressive

- ☐ Sarcasm

- ☐ Verbal abuse

- ☐ Blaming

- ☐ Guerrilla humor

- ☐ Retaliatory anger

- ☐ Blind rage

- ☐ Isolation

- ☐ Depression

- ☐ Others

_____

_____

_____

Expression and Roles of Anger

Objective

To identify the role(s) anger has served.

Materials Needed

Handout – Roles of Anger

Starting Point

Recognizing the role and purpose anger plays in the client's life is an insight-oriented discussion that is helpful to their being empathetic to their anger as a defense. They are not being judged for their anger, nor do they need to judge themselves as people, but to understand their behavior. Using the Roles of Anger handout, offer the following didactic.

Didactic

Recognizing the role and purpose anger has played in your life will help you to identify how it has been reinforced and what new skills you need to replace the role anger has served.

Is your anger a buffer against feelings that you would rather not experience?
Anger can help push away any feelings that frighten you. What is your anger defending or protecting? Do you use anger as a buffer against sadness or disappointment or when you feel helpless or hopeless or guilty? Do you use anger when you do not want people to see your hurt, loneliness, or neediness? Do you use anger to mask fears?

Is your anger a defense against shame?
Shame is the internalized belief that says you are defective, insufficient, or unworthy. Shame is difficult to endure and many defenses are developed against it, rage being one. Enduring attacks on your identity and worth, you develop a barricade around yourself and push your way through life. Rage is a great defense that pushes people away so that they don't get close enough to see what it is you believe to be so ugly. You push people away because you need to defend against the possibility of closeness or rejection.

Do you use anger as a form of self-protection? Do you think others, including those you love, are regularly attempting to humiliate you?
Anger is often used to verbally attack someone before they attack you. You anticipate that you will be slighted in some manner, so to take control of the situation and protect yourself from the perceived incoming attack you attack first — thus thwarting the anticipated offense.

Does anger give you a sense of power?
One of the greatest reinforcements of anger is the feeling of power it gives. The more powerlessness you have experienced, the greater the pull towards anger. It compensates for powerlessness. Momentarily you feel you have gained power, or status over another. A false sense of power it may be, but a false sense of power feels better than no sense of power at all.

Does anger allow you to avoid responsibility?
Anger can be used to avoid responsibility for your choices and actions. If it is all somebody else's fault then you don't have to change. It's easier to think of what they need to do to be different rather than focus on what you could do differently. It is possible that your being different seems so impossible that the thought taps your powerlessness and helplessness which quickly reinforces going back towards the anger, a much safer feeling.

Does anger allow you to feel righteously indignant or morally superior?
Do you take the stance that you have every right to be angry because the world is full of injustices? Your hostility only fuels those injustices even more.

Is anger used as a way to get high?
One can use anger to achieve moments of intensity in an otherwise flat and listless life. It can be a great energizer, a way to get high with excitement, to feel suddenly alive instead of dull or apathetic. You may find yourself seeking out arguments and physical fights because the sense of rage is thrilling and a kind of euphoria sets in. But the rush you derive from anger keeps you angry.

Ask each client to share which roles they identify with and to give examples of situations.

Roles of Anger

Check the roles of anger that you relate to:

☐ Buffer against feelings

☐ Defense against shame

☐ Self-protection

☐ Power

☐ Avoid responsibility

☐ Self-righteousness, moral superiority

☐ Energizer, to get high with excitement, to feel alive

☐ Others

_____

_____

_____

Anger Line

Objectives

To identify anger incidents and behavioral responses.
To recognize anger triggers and patterns.

Materials Needed

Handout – Anger Line
Handout – Anger Avoidant Line
Large pieces of paper (11 x 14 or 14 x 18)
Pens or pencils

Starting Point

Asking clients to create an anger line allows them to reflect on significant situations in which they experienced anger and provides a focused format in which to discuss it.

The point to this exercise is not to identify all anger situations, but to begin to recognize and articulate patterns of triggers and reactions. Chronically angry people become angry at so many things that they can no longer distinguish one situation from another. This exercise will help clients to develop clarity about their anger patterns.

Give each client the handout Anger Line along with a large piece of paper and pen or pencil. Using the handout as an example, ask them to draw a long line with Birth at one end and Today at the other. Above the line note situations or events that angered them and their approximate age at the time. Below the line note what they did in response to the event or situation.

Allow 30 minutes for clients to complete their Anger Line. An alternative is to offer the handout as an assignment thereby giving clients more time for reflection.

Optional Anger Avoidant component: People with anger problems are not always obviously angry. They may go to great lengths to avoid anger only to have it surface in distorted or hostile behaviors. This additional part of the Anger Line exercise will be helpful to clients who have avoidant aspects to their history with anger. Ask clients to draw a second line and this time note events or situations in which they had cause to be angry, but for whatever reasons, i.e. self-protection, a sense of futility, etc. they discounted, minimized or denied their anger; indicate their approximate age and then note what they did or told themselves to mask their anger. Use the handout Anger Avoidant Line as an example.

Anger Line

Example:

Anger events	Grandmother died	Best friend moved	Family dog given away	Parents divorced	Expelled from college	Got divorced	Lost job
Age	7	10	11	15	21	24	36

Birth ——————— Today

What I did	Broke my toys	Ran away from home	Set fire to the doghouse	Stopped talking to my dad	Went out and got drunk	Crashed my car	Stole some equipment from the job

On a large piece of paper draw a line like the one in the example. Above the line note the situations or events that angered you and your approximate age at the time. Underneath the line note what you did with your anger.

You may find yourself continuing to add to the line as discussion leads to even greater memory.

Anger Avoidant Line

Example:

Anger events	Mom stays out late/ doesn't check on us	Dad doesn't send child support	Stepdad calls me names	Brother picks on me	Wife tells me I am stupid & lazy	Didn't get raise I wanted
Age	6+	always	9	9-17	today	today
What I did	Watched TV to distract	Told people my dad was dead	Stole from his coin collection	Stole things from his room	Ignored her & surfed the Internet	Withheld information on work project

Birth ——————————————————————— **Today**

On a large piece of paper draw a line like the one in the example. Above the line note events or situations in which you had cause to be angry but for whatever reason, i.e. to protect yourself, sense of futility, etc., you discounted, minimized, or denied your anger. Indicate your approximate age. Below the line note what you did or told yourself to mask your anger. It can be helpful to use two different color pens or pencils, one for your first Anger Line and another for this one.

You may find yourself continuing to add to the line as discussion leads to even greater memory.

In the Red Zone

Objectives

To identify perception of anger depth.
To recognize the role of family influence.

Materials Needed

Handout – Anger Meter
Handout – Anger Sentence Stem

Starting Point

The handout Anger Meter can either be a written exercise and then discussed or a guide for discussion only. This exercise is a simple but structured opportunity to assist clients to 1) identify their perception of being angry and, 2) to begin the process of recognizing how family and cultural influences have impacted them.

The handout Anger Sentence Stem is an additional tool that will reinforce the understanding of multi-generational repetition. Read some of the examples given in the handout and then instruct clients to complete the sentences spontaneously without editing their thoughts, moving from one sentence stem to another. When completed ask clients to read their sentences aloud and then discuss any new thoughts or awareness this may have evoked.

Anger Meter

In general, I consider myself (mark your level of anger on the meter below):

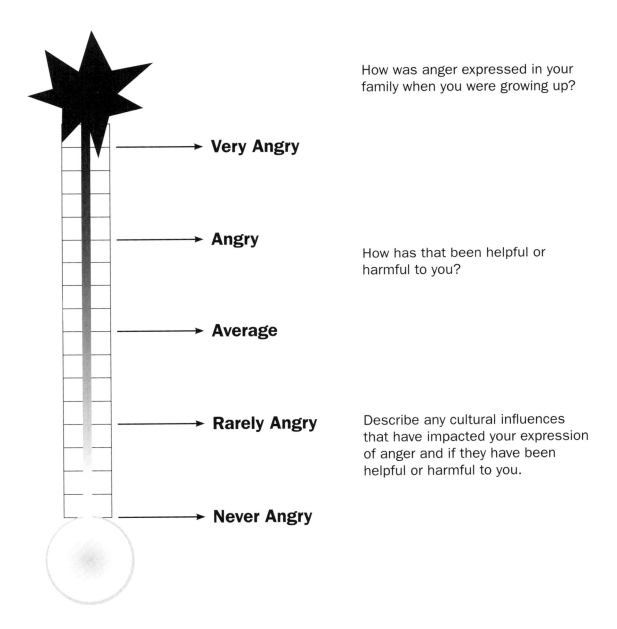

How was anger expressed in your family when you were growing up?

Very Angry

Angry

How has that been helpful or harmful to you?

Average

Rarely Angry

Describe any cultural influences that have impacted your expression of anger and if they have been helpful or harmful to you.

Never Angry

Anger Sentence Stem

Complete the following sentences:

1.
When my dad got angry, he _____

When my dad got angry, he _____

Examples:
When my dad got angry he called us names and swore.
When my dad got angry he would storm out of the house and be gone for hours.

2.
When my dad got angry, I _____

When my dad got angry, I _____

Examples:
When my dad got angry I got really scared.
When my dad got angry I wanted to run and hide.

3.
When my mom got angry, she _____

When my mom got angry, she _____

Examples:
When my mom got angry she would yell and then cry.
When my mom got angry she would slam doors and go to her bedroom.

4.
When my mom got angry, I _____

When my mom got angry, I _____

Examples:
When my mom got angry I felt bad.
When my mom got angry I wanted to make her feel better.

5.
When I got angry at my mom, she _____

When I got angry at my mom, she _____

Examples:
When I got angry at my mom she told me I had no right.
When I got angry at my mom she told me I was ungrateful.

6.
When I got angry at my dad, he _____

When I got angry at my dad, he _____

Examples:
When I got angry at my dad he never knew it.
When I got angry at my dad I would take it out on my brother.

7.
Today when I get angry, I _____

Today when I get angry, I _____

Examples:
Today when I get angry I slam doors and yell.
Today when I get angry I light up a joint.

Anger Collage

Objective

To facilitate discussion of experiences often defended and not recognized in traditional talk therapy.

Materials Needed

Collage materials for each client:
3 to 5 magazines (nearly any magazine can be used; it is suggested that there be an assortment)
14" x 17" pieces of paper, scotch tape, scissors

Starting Point

A collage is a valuable exercise for clients who are well defended through verbal skills or have difficulty saying anything. Ask clients to reflect on their growing up years and create a collage of anger. The collage will vary depending on the direction you orient them toward. Consider directing them toward making a collage of anger in general or their anger or anger in their family.

A collage is made by taking pictures, words, and/or letters from magazines to make a statement. Depending on time, offer clients 20 to 30 minutes to create their collage. Suggest they begin their collage by flipping through a magazine while being open and receptive to what they see rather than looking for specific words or pictures. Part of the value of creating a collage is finding words or pictures that jump out at them and describe their feelings.

These directions are purposely broad. This gives clients the opportunity to describe the anger of others or themselves, the cause of the anger, and how the anger was expressed.

It is more effective to not offer examples unless clients seem confused about the assignment. The following are examples that, if needed, may be helpful.

A picture of…

1. a volcano may represent how explosive and frightening it was when your dad got angry.
2. a car may represent terrifying rides with an angry parent.
3. a table set for dinner may represent all the family dinners where no one spoke a word because of the fear of provoking anger.
4. the word Dad may represent the only one in the family allowed to be angry.
5. a woman in tears may represent how you expressed your anger.

The Family Gift

Objectives

To recognize familial influence on unhealthy anger.
To be accountable for hurtful behavior.

Materials Needed

Handout – Identifying Unjust Anger
Board

Starting Point

The single most common cause of unhealthy anger is being raised in a home filled with unhealthy expressions of anger. Children learn how they should be angry from their parents. Families in which there is chronic anger think that a lot of anger is normal and expected; that nobody listens until someone gets angry. They try to solve all of their problems with anger. Unhealthy anger becomes the norm and is repeated generationally.

List on a board examples of unhealthy expressions of anger such as:

name calling	caustic humor	sarcasm
verbal put downs	pushing, shoving	kicking
swearing	threats	hyper criticism
silence as punishment	biting	other

Using the handout Identifying Unjust Anger, ask clients to write out their own examples of being the recipient of other peoples' hurtful anger, and examples of themselves perpetuating unjust anger toward others. It is suggested the handout be used as a model and that additional paper is available to clients so as to allow for more extensive self-disclosure.

The purpose of identifying unjust family anger is not to place blame on the family for clients' present-day hurtful behaviors, but to recognize where such behaviors were learned and assist in the process of clients sharing their vulnerability as children.

As clients own their behavior, it may be helpful to assist them in preventing a shame attack. (See Section Two: Shame Attacks, page 55) Reinforce with clients that this is about their behaviors and not about them as individuals.

Indentifying Unjust Anger

Example:

Person Directing Anger	My Age	Anger Behavior
Grandfather	7-10	Beat me with a strap
Brother	Baby to 15	Hit me/tied me up/shut me in the closet
Dad	12-15	Ignored me/threatened to beat me
Stepdad	17	Called me "good for nothing"/refused to take me places but took my brother
Wife	34	Verbal abuse/silence

Part 1:

Note the names of persons who directed their anger at you, your approximate age at the time, and the specific form of anger that was directed at you.

Person Directing Anger	My Age	Anger Behavior

Part 2:

Identify persons who have been the recipient of your unjust anger and your specific anger behavior towards them.

Recipient of My Anger	Anger Behavior

Cognitive Strategies

Overview of
Cognitive Strategies

Cognitive therapy is an essential treatment modality in addressing anger. The client with anger issues frequently reacts from faulty and distorted thinking. This section offers a variety of specific tools to challenge cognitive distortions and instill new ways of perceiving events that allow for healthier responses to a situation.

Differing Perceptions is an invaluable exercise that demonstrates how several persons' perception of the same event varies tremendously depending upon a person's history, expectation, and intent.

Distorted Thinking will help clients explore and identify faulty and negative thinking patterns. It will give them an opportunity to be accountable for their own distortions and develop skills to intervene in self-defeating thought patterns.

Beliefs challenges the negative thoughts and beliefs that fuel anger and provides clients the opportunity to recognize how old beliefs do not serve them well. Reframing beliefs is crucial in supporting new healthier behavior.

Shame is a foundational core belief that propels the inappropriate expression of anger. Having an understanding of the development of shame and being able to identify shame-based behaviors is a significant step in lessening self-defeating behaviors.

Shame Attacks offers a technique to stop the perpetuation of shame-based beliefs, negative self-talk, and self-defeating behaviors.

Anger Awareness Cycle is a critical strategy in helping clients recognize and intervene in their own anger processes. This tool is useful as a reference throughout the therapeutic process.

Thoughts — Emotions — Behaviors will help clients recognize how change in thinking creates change in feelings and, consequently, change in behavior. This is another tool that can be referred to and practiced during the treatment process.

Degrees of Anger facilitates the identification of anger along a continuum. By identifying different degrees of anger clients can learn to intervene in less intense anger moments and have a broader vocabulary to talk about their feelings.

Differing Perceptions

Objective

To heighten awareness of how thoughts influence feelings.

Materials Needed

Board

Starting Point

The perception of an event is a personal experience and each interpretation is reality to the viewer. Yet clearly peoples' thinking patterns influence their emotional experience. This exercise assists in making that point.

Describe the following event for clients to demonstrate that depending upon the person, his or her experience of the event and the feelings associated with it will vary greatly. Creating a visual of this discussion through the use of a board is helpful in making an impact.

A snowstorm:

Person	Thought	Feeling
Child	School is canceled	Happiness
Dad	Won't get home from work	Disappointment
Elderly Person	I could easily fall down	Fear
	My grandchildren will be able to visit because school will be canceled	Happiness
Mail Carrier	I will never finish my route	Frustration
	My truck could get stuck	Anger

Continue with this model of discussion and use of the board. Ask clients to respond to the following events by identifying thoughts and associated feelings that might occur:

Plane crash —

1. president of the airline company
2. the sole survivor
3. a witness to the crash
4. the first official to arrive at the scene
5. a television viewer

Day after Thanksgiving — the busiest shopping day of the year —

1. an avid shopper
2. a store security guard
3. a store clerk
4. a store owner
5. a delivery driver

Offer other examples relevant to your clients' lives, i.e.—

- Your new coworker passes you in the hall without saying hello.
- Your son doesn't answer the phone when you call home at a time you would expect him to be there.
- Your spouse hasn't done the laundry and the clothes that you wanted to wear are not clean.

Distorted Thinking

Objectives

To identify distorted thinking styles.
To develop a rational response to replace distorted thinking.

Materials Needed

Handout – Distorted Thinking Styles

Starting Point

People who engage in negative and distorted thinking do so without recognizing how they create self-defeating thought patterns and behaviors.

Didactic

There are several ways people distort and engage in negative thinking.

Overestimating — Overestimating the odds of a bad outcome. "If I go to the reunion, I know my brother will pick a fight."

Filtering — Selecting and focusing on one negative aspect of a situation so that the positive aspects are ignored. "I didn't do that good in the competition, so what is the point of continuing?"

Overgeneralization — Jumping from one instance in the present to all instances in the future. "My husband doesn't love me. I will always be alone."

Mind-Reading — Basing assumptions and conclusions on your ability to know other people's thoughts. "I know he doesn't like me. I can tell by the way he looks at me."

Catastrophizing — Turning everything into a catastrophe, always expecting the worse case scenario. "My son is doing poorly in school. I doubt that he will ever graduate."

Personalization — Interpreting everything around you in ways that reflect on you and your self-worth. "My coworkers were laughing outside my work station. I know they were making fun of me."

Disqualifying the Positive — Rejecting positive experiences by insisting they don't count. "She was being nice to me, but I know that she didn't really mean it."

Fairness Fallacy — Falling into the trap of judging people's actions by rules that you have concocted about what is and what isn't fair. "If I work hard they will owe me a raise."

Blaming — Believing that the hurtful things that happen are someone else's fault. "I wouldn't have lost my temper with you had you been home when you said you would be."

Shoulds — Operating from a rigid set of self-imposed rules about how everyone, including you should act. "I should be totally self-reliant."

The following exercise helps clients to recognize their patterns so that they can stop the hurtful thinking and recreate or reframe more rational and healthier thinking styles.

In a discussion, ask clients to identify examples of distorted thinking styles using those identified on the handout Distorted Thinking Styles. If working with a group, ask the group for two examples of each style, then have each person complete the handout for themselves. If working with an individual review the different styles and then ask the client to complete the handout.

After discussion and when the handout is completed, review and select three styles of thinking that they and/or you, the facilitator, see as the most disruptive in their lives and explore the following questions for each style selected:

How do you feel when employing this style of thinking?

How has it caused conflict between you and others?

What is a rational response to replace the distorted thinking?

Assist them in any of the areas they have difficulty developing a rational response to stop distorted thinking.

It's easy for clients to catch themselves in distorted thinking by remembering to be vigilant to their use of words such as never, always, all, everyone, no one, and none. These are all words spoken in absolutes as if there is no other possibility. Other words such as worthless, stupid, false, hopeless, pointless, and unfair are also strong indicators that one is engaged in distorted thinking.

By listing examples of cognitive distortion in a visible place for clients to readily see, developing awareness can be an ongoing process. When someone speaks or thinks a negative thought, the thinker or the listener rings a bell (or similar device). This is a fun concrete activity to develop a user-friendly "stop thought" technique. Ask the person who offered the thought to identify what he or she was doing, i.e., catastrophizing, blaming, etc. Then you can assist your clients with counterthoughts.

Distorted Thinking Styles

Negative thinking can be identified as distorted thinking. Give two examples for each style you identify with.

Overestimating:
Overestimating the odds of a bad outcome. "If I go to the reunion, I know my brother will pick a fight."

 1. _____

 2. _____

Filtering:
Selecting and focusing on one negative aspect of a situation so that the positive aspects are ignored. "I didn't do that good in the competition, so what is the point of continuing?"

 1. _____

 2. _____

Overgeneralization:
Jumping from one instance in the present to all instances in the future. "My husband doesn't love me. I will always be alone."

 1. _____

 2. _____

Mind-Reading:
Basing assumptions and conclusions on your ability to know other people's thoughts. "I know he doesn't like me. I can tell by the way he looks at me."

 1. _____

 2. _____

Catastrophizing:
Turning everything into a catastrophe, always expecting the worse case scenario. "My son is doing poorly in school. I doubt that he will ever graduate."

 1. _____

 2. _____

Personalization:

Interpreting everything around you in ways that reflect on you and your self-worth. "My coworkers were laughing outside my work station. I know they were making fun of me."

1. _____
2. _____

Disqualifying the Positive:

Rejecting positive experiences by insisting they don't count. "She was being nice to me, but I know that she didn't really mean it.

1. _____
2. _____

Fairness Fallacy:

Falling into the trap of judging people's actions by rules that you have concocted about what is and what isn't fair. "If I work hard they will owe me a raise."

1. _____
2. _____

Blaming:

Believing that bad hurtful things that happen are someone else's fault. "I wouldn't have lost my temper with you had you been home when you said you would be."

1. _____
2. _____

Shoulds:

Operating from a rigid set of self-imposed rules about how everyone, including you should act. "I should be totally self-reliant."

1. _____
2. _____

Now ask yourself:

How did it feel when using that distorted thinking?

How has it caused conflict between myself and others?

What would be a rational comeback to replace that distorted thinking?

Distorted Thinking

Beliefs

Objectives

To identify negative beliefs that fuel anger.
To recognize negative beliefs stem from antiquated systems.
To reframe beliefs in a positive way.

Materials Needed

Handout – Beliefs That Fuel Anger

Starting Point

Using the handout Beliefs That Fuel Anger ask clients to identify which beliefs fuel their negative expression of anger then to reflect on where they think this belief originated.

One by one go through each belief on the handout. Ask clients to share as a group if they identified and to discuss the belief's original source.

After the sharing of where their beliefs originated, take one or two beliefs and work with helping clients to see how the gross generalization of a belief is not valid, i.e. "You can't trust anyone." Ask them as a group to generate ideas of situations in which they did trust someone. List the many examples that will come forth.

Questions that may facilitate ideas:

Who can you trust to provide transportation to work when your car breaks down?

Who do you trust has the ability to fix it?

Who can you trust to loan you $10 when you ask?

Who do you trust that you can tell a particular problem to?

The goal is to help them see how they generalize from the pain that is associated with an experience, such as a time during which they really wanted to rely on someone and that person didn't come through. The disappointment or embarrassment was so painful that they created a belief that was meant to be self-protective: "I won't trust anyone. People are not trustworthy."

Ask them what negative consequences they experience for this belief today.

Another belief is: "I can't do anything about my anger. It's just me."
To counteract that polarized belief, ask them to identify times in which they became out of control with their anger but, in hindsight, it could have become worse. In fact, they did show some ability to stop and demonstrate control.

Example:

A man at work is so fed up with his supervisor, he gets angry and takes his boss by the front of his shirt and shoves him against the wall. He yells and threatens him but finally just stops and walks away. In hindsight, he could have hit him. As out of control as he felt, he could have been more out of control. In fact, he had the wherewithal to stop his attack and walk away.

Continue to reinforce the negative consequences for anger and how anger is directly related to one's belief system. As clients identify where their belief systems originated it is appropriate to validate their experience.

For this session, keep the focus on their most predominant beliefs and guide them in recognizing the pattern of all-or-nothing thinking.

Prior to the close of this session spend time asking clients to review the handout and create new beliefs to counteract negative beliefs. They will reframe these beliefs to be more constructive, e.g. "Anger never hurt anybody," is rewritten as: "Anger, expressed wrong, hurts many people."

Beliefs That Fuel Anger

What are the beliefs that fuel your anger? As an act of taking ownership of your belief system, identify those beliefs and ascertain whether they are hurtful or helpful to how you want to live your life today. The following are common anger-fueling beliefs. Check those you identify with and add others to that list. With those you checked, indicate what factor(s) helped to influence that belief. Recreate a new belief that demonstrates a healthier way of thinking.

Beliefs	What factors influenced your belief?	New Belief
☐ People are out to get me.		
☐ You can't trust anyone.		
☐ Take advantage before being taken advantage of.		
☐ They don't really like me.		
☐ They are being nice only because they have to.		
☐ I am not responsible. It's somebody else's fault.		
☐ I can't do anything about my anger. It's just me.		
☐ Anger never hurt anybody.		
☐ I am just an angry person.		
☐ Other		

Shame

Objectives

To understand the origins of shame.
To understand the relationship between shame and anger.
To challenge self-defeating messages.

Materials Needed

Handout – Shaming Messages
Board

Starting Point

Psychologists and philosophers frequently refer to healthy and unhealthy shame. Healthy shame is experienced with humility and conscience. Unhealthy shame erodes one's self-confidence, telling one that one is inadequate, insufficient, less than. Unhealthy shame is often integral to angry behavior. Anger is the mask to this shame and a client's angry behavior casts shame toward the victim of his or her anger.

Didactic

Unhealthy shame can be identified as the feeling that comes with a personal belief that says, "I am not adequate. I am insufficient, I am damaged." Or thinking of yourself as a mistake, stupid, incompetent, unworthy, damaged goods. Unhealthy shame is learned and most frequently begins in the family environment. As a child, it is paramount in developing healthy esteem to experience your preciousness and have your value mirrored back to you through your parents' words and actions. If you were raised in a troubled family and your parents or caretakers were unable to fill this essential need, it is likely that you internalized beliefs of not being good enough or that you were unlovable. When your core needs were not met; when you were the recipient of shaming messages such as, "You are so stupid," "You'll never amount to anything," you began to internalize the message that there was something flawed with your being.

With its overt and covert messages, society also helps to reinforce your inner shame core. Society constantly bombards you with messages about how you are supposed to look, where to live, what to drive, how to act, etc. When you do not live up to these societal standards, you are shamed by society.

Intolerance to differences, racism, homophobia, and bigotry fuel shame. If you have a source of self-esteem and caregivers who help you to cope with injustices and unhealthy messages, shame is not necessarily learned.

Shame is often the very core of your angry behavior. You turn to anger to feel better. This becomes a never-ending cycle. You feel shame; you mask it with anger, often feeling more shame because of your angry behavior. Until you are able to address the shame it will persist and pose an ever-present threat to your recovery. If people grow up with shame-based messages directed towards them they learn to shame themselves. If you were told you were stupid, it is likely that today you tell yourself you are stupid. If you were shamed because of your weight, it is likely that today you shame yourself for your weight.

It is important to address the shaming messages you hear from others and the shaming messages you give to yourself. By doing this you raise your awareness of how these messages may be automatic to you. When they occur, you need specific tools to address these shaming messages.

Ask clients to give two or three examples of shaming statements they heard as they were growing up. Have them complete the handout Shaming Messages and then discuss it.

Continue the discussion by asking clients to identify shame-producing and/or self-defeating statements they make to themselves. These are often spoken in absolutes, as if fact.

Examples are:

"I am not good enough."

"I will never get my life together."

"I'll never get this job done, so why try?"

If they have difficulty getting started, choose areas of their lives for them to focus on such as self-defeating messages related to school, work, relationships, children, etc. Write their examples on a board and address each self-defeating message individually by asking:

Is this thought productive or counterproductive?

How uncomfortable does this thought make you feel?

How does this thought interfere with your life?

Does this thought support your goals or detract from your goals?

After discussion, encourage clients to pay attention to when they hear themselves making such statements and to employ a STOP message the minute they become aware of what they are saying to themselves. Then ask themselves the questions just posed.

Shaming Messages

1) Give examples of shaming messages you heard when growing up. *"You're stupid", "dumb", "ugly."*

_____

_____

_____

_____

_____

_____

_____

2) Give examples of shaming behaviors you experienced. *Parents yelling at you in a public place; being made to stand in the corner for unreasonable periods of time.*

_____

_____

_____

_____

_____

_____

_____

3) Give examples of how you see those shaming messages/behaviors present in your life today. *Yelling at my own children in a public place; telling others they are stupid and incompetent; being afraid of making a mistake; thinking others are smarter than I am; not trying things I'd like to do.*

_____

_____

_____

_____

_____

_____

_____

Shame Attacks

Objective

To understand shame attacks and to intervene in this negative process.

Materials Needed

Handout – Recovery from Shame Attacks

Starting Point

Addressing shame-based thinking is an extension of and a specific focus on distorted thinking. Distorted thinking styles are integral to shame attacks. This type of thinking engages one in self-disparaging thoughts furthering the erosion of self-esteem. With the erosion of self-esteem comes more distorted thoughts, thus the process becomes cyclical. The following information will help clients to understand and recognize their shame inducing thinking.

Didactic

When you grow up in a dysfunctional environment filled with shaming messages and behaviors, your core belief that you are flawed is ever present. So, when in stressful situations or when someone displays shaming behavior toward you or gives you a shaming message, you may experience what is called a Shame Attack. A Shame Attack occurs when your internal negative beliefs that you are inadequate, stupid, ugly, or incompetent are re-engaged. You often feel like a young child again; defenseless, abandoned, terrified because it recreates the trauma you experienced in the past.

Shame Attacks incorporate catastrophizing. An example of a Shame Attack is:
"I made a mistake in my finances and I bounced a check. Since I bounced this check, I'll probably bounce many more, I will have to declare bankruptcy and then my credit will be ruined." From this catastrophizing, it's then very easy to start to shame yourself by saying, "I really am stupid and I can't do anything right."

Another example of a Shame Attack is:
You are expected to present the culmination of a project at work tomorrow. You have worked diligently but today you heard a co-worker's very fine presentation. You compare yourself to this co-worker and begin to feel incompetent, stupid, and incapable of presenting as well. You then "catastrophize" the situation, saying to yourself, "I will lose my job. They will be sorry they hired me," and on and on.

Ask clients if they can identify with the concept of a Shame Attack and to give examples.

In recovery, it is extremely important to learn how to get out of a Shame Attack. If you are experiencing a Shame Attack, you need to:

- **Identify it for what it is.**

This is a Shame Attack. I am feeling less than, and catastrophizing (only seeing the worst).

- **Stop the thinking.**
- **Check the reality.**

Look at the previous two examples. What is the reality here?

> **Check bouncing situation**
> ***Reality:*** you bounced a check. You made an error in your arithmetic. You were stressed and weren't thinking when you wrote the check. Most people will bounce a check sometime. You can call the payee the check was made to and tell them of your plan for repayment.

> **Fear of presenting work project**
> ***Reality:*** you feel insecure. Another person made a good presentation. You have worked hard on this but are anxious. You want your superior to be impressed. None of this means you are incompetent. It says you are anxious. Past experience indicates your confidence shows once you begin your presentation.

- **Get outside feedback.**
  In a Shame Attack you are distorting the reality. You have lost sight of what is real and true and revert to fear.

- **Look at the origin of the shaming statement.**
  This is another important long-term tool in stopping a Shame Attack. After you've garnered a more realistic perspective, ask yourself, "What were the harsh words I used against myself?" They were usually words such as "I am stupid." "I can't do anything right." When did you first come to believe those messages about yourself?

In the previous session clients were encouraged to note self-deprecating statements they made throughout the day. When they spoke harshly to themselves, they were perpetuating a Shame Attack. Take a few examples from clients and with each message they gave themselves, ask them to stop and reflect on where that message originated.

Example:
> "I'm so stupid I can't get anything right."
> **Stop:** Where did you first hear that?
> **Answer:** My dad.

Now direct clients to give an example of their statement not being true, the purpose being to get them out of a shaming statement.

Example:

> "I'll never amount to anything."
> **Stop:** Where did you first hear that?
> **Answer:** My mother.
> **Example of this not being true:** I now own my own business.

In a Shame Attack, you may feel the vulnerability of a child, often because you were shamed at a young age when indeed you were vulnerable. So when you experience an attack, talk yourself into your stronger adult reality.

Shaming statements come from outside of you. You were not born with shaming messages or toxic shame; they had to be given to you. You were told these things by your parents, caregivers, relatives, spouse/partner, or society. So when experiencing a Shame Attack, you need to recognize that the message comes from outside of yourself.

Offer the handout Recovery from Shame Attacks for clients to use as a tool for stopping Shame Attacks.

Recovery from Shame Attacks

- **Identify it for what it is.**
  This is a Shame Attack. I am feeling less than…and catastrophizing (only seeing the worst).

- **Stop the thinking.**

- **Check the reality.**

  Check bouncing situation
  Reality: you bounced a check. You made an error in your arithmetic. You were stressed and weren't thinking when you wrote the check.
  Reality: most people will bounce a check sometime.
  Reality: you can call the payee the check was made to and tell them of your plan for repayment.

  Fear of presenting work project
  Reality: you feel insecure. Another person made a good presentation. You have worked hard on this but are anxious. You want your superior to be impressed. None of this means you are incompetent. It says you are anxious. Past experience says your confidence shows once you begin your presentation.

- **Get outside feedback.**
  In a Shame Attack you are distorting the reality. You have lost sight of what is real and true and revert to fear.

- **Look at the origin of the shaming statement.**
  This is another important long-term tool in stopping a Shame Attack. After you've garnered a more realistic perspective, ask yourself: What were the harsh words I used against myself? They are usually words such as "I am stupid and I can't do anything right." When did you first come to believe those messages about yourself?

Anger Awareness Cycle

Objective

To recognize the cycle of the anger process.

Materials Needed

Handout – Awareness Cycle
Handout – Anger Cycle Diary
Board

Starting Point

The Anger Awareness Cycle originally created by Gestalt therapists Polster, Polster and Zinker describes a naturally occurring sequence that consists of five major components:

1. Awareness — initial awareness of a sensation, emotion or thought

2. Focus — serves to focus the sensation, emotion or thought

3. Action — excitement is transformed into behavior

4. Feedback — internal and external feedback on that behavior

5. Withdrawal — energy and interest is withdrawn from that concern

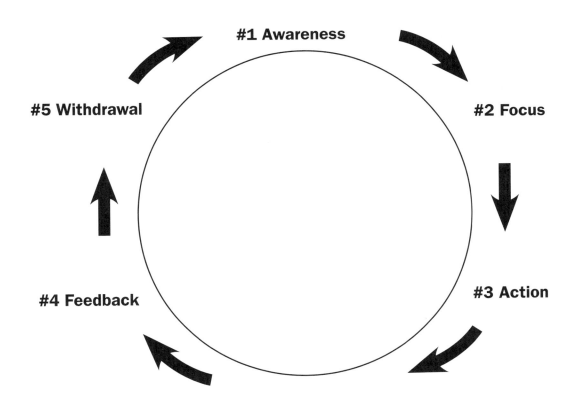

Draw an awareness cycle on the board. Give clients the handouts Chronically Angry and Anger Cycle Diary and share the following information.

Didactic

Anger is one of many signals that there is something wrong in your life. You need to utilize your initial awareness of anger to discover the nature of the problem and its solution. You don't want to run away from legitimate concerns avoiding anger, or hanging on to anger when it has served its purpose. You want to listen to it, choose whether to act on it and how, and then withdraw your investment in being angry.

Look at the awareness cycle in these examples:

(1) Awareness
Someone is thirsty, begins to lick their lips but ignores the thirst and stays focused on whatever else they were doing.

(2) Focus
Soon, they lick their lips again, and again they ignore it, but the next time they lick their lips they cannot ignore it.

(3) Action
Aware that their thirst is not going away, they pour a glass of water and drink it.

(4) Feedback
They taste the water, feel the coolness of it in their mouth, and feel a sense of physical relief.

(5) Withdrawal
Their interest moves on to something else.

Another example:

(1) Awareness
You find out that a colleague has made a decision that affects you but he/she failed to talk to you about it first.

(2) Focus
You let it pass, but a couple hours later you're thinking about it again and soon find yourself angry and preoccupied thinking about it.

(3) Action
You confront the person directly; ask if what you heard is accurate; tell them how this impacts you.

(4) Feedback
The internal feedback is what you feel and think for having been assertive and when you hear what the other person has to say.

(5) Withdrawal
You now have the option of letting go of your anger and moving on to something else.

Chronic anger is a pattern of thinking, acting, and feeling in which a person seeks or embraces and/or prolongs anger experiences. The chronically angry person gets mad too easily, stays mad too long, and misuses or misdirects the anger. This person is all too ready to find reasons to become irritated, irate, or enraged — is oversensitive to anger cues, and under-sensitive to cues for other feelings — ignores invitations to joy, sadness, fear, etc., to concentrate only on noticing anger opportunities.

The **chronically angry person's** anger quickly moves from (1) Awareness to (2) Focus, becoming concentrated and intensified, or moves from (1) Awareness to (3) Action with no (2) Focus on or contemplation of the situation. This is someone who escalates into blind rage, springing into impulsive or exaggerated anger. By this time, if a rage response has been triggered, it is difficult for this person to take in any external (4) Feedback at all.

Conversely, this person's immediate internal (4) Feedback is often quite positive, an anger high, a sense of feeling alive. It is only later that he or she may feel regret and remorse.

Studies of anger in children indicate that their internal processes simply take over during a rage. Children cannot be comforted at these times because they are so involved with their feelings. All that can be done for them is to keep them safe until they regain touch with the world.

A similar process may occur whenever chronically angry adults fly into a rage. For a short period of time these persons cannot listen to reason because their ability to reason is sublimated by their feelings. This is why the only effective tactic to use on these occasions is a time out. (Remind clients how time outs work as described in the Instructions.)

For the chronically angry person, (5) Withdrawal presents a problem, as they cannot or will not withdraw, and they cling to their anger. They brood over past insults and slights, or they develop strong resentments as they dwell on old problems. They have a tendency to refuse to move beyond the anger; to do so would mean giving up the anger and that would force this person to become aware of other feelings.

The **anger avoidant person** moves counter-clockwise in the awareness cycle. He or she will go out of the way to not recognize any form of anger, and will rationalize, discount, and move into (5) Withdrawal at the first hint of anger. Should they move to the (2) Focus stage, they do what they can to move to (5) Withdrawal. If they (3) Act on their anger, they often quickly experience the internal (4) Feedback of guilt and remorse, seeing their self as a bad person for upsetting another. At all times they want to (5) Withdraw from their anger.

Whereas you may not identify with being anger avoidant, it is helpful to understand the opposite of the cycle because there is a tendency to jump from being chronically angry to the all-or-nothing response of anger avoidance. It is also common for chronically angry people to choose a spouse/partner who is anger avoidant.

Neither the chronically angry position, nor the anger avoidant position allows the person to use the human feeling of anger in a healthy, positive constructive manner.

Utilizing the handout Awareness Cycle, ask clients to give two examples of how they move in the anger cycle. If they are not able to do this, give feedback as to how you see them move through this process.

The handout Anger Cycle Diary is an excellent tool for clients to remain vigilant to their particular process. In numbers 1 through 5 on the handout, the (a) response is the goal; (b) is indicative of avoidant anger; and (c) is indicative of chronic anger. Using clients' personal examples, review the handout with them prior to having them complete it as an assignment.

Awareness Cycle

Chronically Angry Position

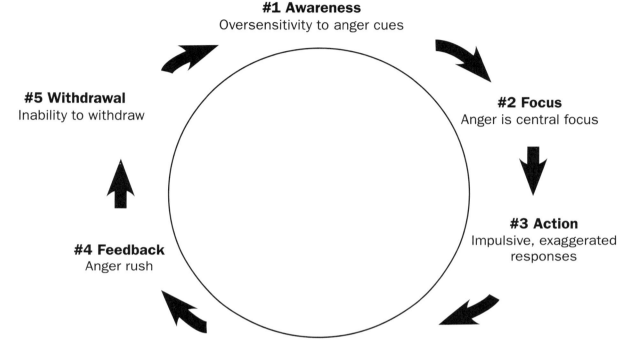

#1 Awareness
Oversensitivity to anger cues

#5 Withdrawal
Inability to withdraw

#2 Focus
Anger is central focus

#4 Feedback
Anger rush

#3 Action
Impulsive, exaggerated responses

Anger Avoidant Position

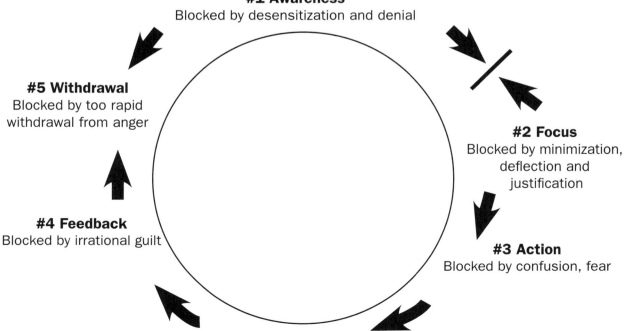

#1 Awareness
Blocked by desensitization and denial

#5 Withdrawal
Blocked by too rapid withdrawal from anger

#2 Focus
Blocked by minimization, deflection and justification

#4 Feedback
Blocked by irrational guilt

#3 Action
Blocked by confusion, fear

66

Anger Cycle Diary

Description of the Anger Incident: _____
_____
_____
_____

1. In this incident, I (a) noticed; (b) ignored; (c) looked for my angry feelings in the following way(s):
_____
_____
_____

2. In this incident, I (a) focused on; (b) minimized; (c) emphasized my anger in the following way(s):
_____
_____
_____

3. In this incident, I (a) took a reasonable action; (b) did not act; (c) acted impulsively on my angry feelings in the following way(s):
_____
_____
_____

4. In this incident, I (a) shared my anger clearly and tactfully; (b) felt badly about sharing my anger; (c) had a strong rush of anger and liked expressing it, in the following way(s):
_____
_____
_____

5. In this incident, I (a) let go of my anger as soon as the problem was resolved; (b) guiltily took back my anger as soon as I could; (c) hung on to my anger and resentment even after I expressed it. Explain:
_____
_____
_____

6. Now that I have had time to think more about this incident, I can tell myself:
_____
_____
_____

7. The main thing that I will do to change how I deal with my anger in the future is:
_____
_____
_____

Source: Anger, Alcoholism, and Addiction by Ronald and Patricia Potter-Efron

Thoughts – Emotions – Behaviors

Objectives

To identify how change in thought influences change in feelings and behavior.
To identify how change in behavior can create change in thoughts and feelings.

Materials Needed

Handout – Thoughts — Emotions — Behaviors

Starting Point

Angry people often say, "I didn't know I was angry until I exploded. I don't know what triggered it." Yet in hindsight there are thoughts, emotions or behaviors that precede intense feelings of anger that influence whether or not people get angry, how angry they become and what they do with their anger.

Using the handout Thoughts—Emotions—Behaviors, present the first two examples given of the relationship between thoughts, emotions, and behaviors.

Ask clients to think back to one of their more recent verbal assaults or explosive behaviors and reflect on the following questions:

What were you doing and what happened to you right before you were verbally assaultive?

What were your thoughts just before that moment?

What was going on inside of you (feelings)?

Ask the questions slowly so that they have the opportunity to reflect. Then elicit from the clients two to three examples of recent verbal assaults or explosive behaviors. Using those examples, walk them through the process offered in the handout to demonstrate how change of thought or behavior creates a more positive outcome.

Ask clients to identify their own examples and using the format on the handout, to project how with a change of thought or behavior the outcome can be more positive.

Ask them to be vigilant to angry circumstances between now and the next session and attempt a change in those circumstances by changing their thoughts or behaviors.

Thoughts—Emotions—Behaviors Worksheet

Thought processes strongly influence your feelings and your behavior. This exercise demonstrates a method to lessen the escalation of anger and promote a greater likelihood of constructive problem solving.

Think back to a recent verbal assault or explosive behavior and ask yourself:

What was I doing, and what happened right before I verbally exploded?

What were my thoughts just before that moment?

What was going on inside me (feelings)?

Example #1:

At work you see your boss talking to one of your coworkers, they are smiling and it appears to be a friendly conversation.

Look at the thoughts or behaviors that would have changed this situation.

Thought #1: "Gee, what are they talking about?"
Feeling #1: curiosity, anxiety
Behavior #1: You keep working, but look over at them frequently.

Thought #1: "Gee, what are they talking about?"
Feeling #1: curiosity, anxiety
Behavior #1: You keep working, but look over at them frequently.

Thought #2: "They're acting too cordial. That guy must've been offered the job I want."
Feeling #2: fearfulness
Behavior #2: You stand still watching them, foot tapping.

Thought #2: "They're acting too cordial. That guy must've been offered the job I want."
Feeling #2: fearfulness
Behavior #2: You stand still watching them, foot tapping.

Thought #3: "My boss is a two-timing no-good. You can't trust anyone. The world isn't fair!"
Feeling #3: anger
Behavior #3: You walk away, go out to your car and sit in it with music blaring.

Thought #3: **CHANGES TO: "I can't hear what they're saying, so I don't know what they are talking about.**
Feeling #3: **CHANGES TO: anxiety**
Behavior #3: **CHANGES TO: You resume work**

Thought #4: "I'm going to quit this job!" or "I don't know why I thought I could ever get anywhere here."
Feeling #4: rage, shame
Behavior #4: You leave work. Yell at parking attendant. Refuse to talk with your spouse/partner and backhand your son for being ten minutes late.

Thought #4: **CHANGES TO: "I need to check this out. I would really like the job."**
Feeling #4: **CHANGES TO: less anxiety**
Behavior #4: **CHANGES TO: When the other person leaves you approach your boss to get clarification regarding your fears.**

Example #2:

You receive a notice from your bank saying you owe money.

Thought #1: "Oh no, not another money problem to deal with."

Feeling #1: fearfulness

Behavior #1: You don't read the notice in full and call the bank.

Thought #2: "Those stupid people! They can't do anything right."

Feeling #2: anger

Behavior #2: You tell the person at the bank they are wrong and incompetent.

Look at the thoughts or behaviors that would have changed this situation.

Thought #1: "Oh no, not another money problem to deal with."

Feeling #1: fearfulness

Behavior #1: **CHANGES TO: You sit down and read the notice carefully.**

Thought #2: **CHANGES TO: "I hope they're wrong. Maybe it's not as bad as I think."**

Feeling #2: **CHANGES TO: anxiety**

Behavior #2: **CHANGES TO: You call the bank and ask if there has been a mistake.**

Think of an example of one of your recent verbal assaults or explosive behaviors and identify your thoughts, feelings, and behavior.

Situation:

Thought #1:

Feeling #1:

Behavior #1:

Thought #2:

Feeling #2:

Behavior #2:

Thought #3:

Feeling #3:

Behavior #3:

Identify the thoughts or behaviors that would have changed this situation.

Thought #1: **CHANGES TO:**

Feeling #1: **CHANGES TO:**

Behavior #1: **CHANGES TO:**

Thought #2: **CHANGES TO:**

Feeling #2: **CHANGES TO:**

Behavior #2: **CHANGES TO:**

Thought #3: **CHANGES TO:**

Feeling #3: **CHANGES TO:**

Behavior #3: **CHANGES TO:**

Thoughts — Emotions — Behaviors

Degrees of Anger

Objective

To recognize varying degrees of anger.

Materials Needed

Handout – Anger Intensity
Board

Starting Point

Anger is often the only safe feeling for the chronically angry person. But it is typically only identified as one feeling versus a variety of feelings along a continuum. Recognizing different degrees of anger will facilitate clients in not always being engaged in a locked emotional state.

Write the following words on a board:

Annoyed	Irritated	Frustrated
Disgusted	Aggravated	Mad
Angry	Furious	Enraged

Facilitator may add words to this list, but remember that the purpose of this exercise is to represent a continuum. Using these words, ask clients to offer examples that reflect how they distinguish between the different levels of anger.

Lead a discussion in problem solving appropriate actions when clients recognize themselves experiencing less intense anger. Failure to recognize lesser degrees of anger drives them from initial awareness of anger into impulsive actions/reactions.

Give clients the handout Anger Intensity as an assignment for them to note situations that come up between this session and the next wherein they can distinguish different levels of anger. This is not to encourage them to create an angry situation, but to recognize the varying degrees of this feeling as it is experienced.

Anger Intensity

In the course of a day or week, identify situations where you distinguish the different intensities of your anger.

Use one of these key words to describe your anger:

1. Annoyed	4. Disgusted	7. Angry
2. Irritated	5. Aggravated	8. Furious
3. Frustrated	6. Mad	9. Enraged

Situation or Event

Example: My wife left dirty dishes in the sink.

_____

_____

_____

_____

_____

_____

_____

_____

_____

_____

_____

_____

Degree of Anger

Disgusted

_____

_____

_____

_____

_____

_____

_____

_____

_____

_____

_____

_____

Behavioral Strategies

Overview of
Behavioral Strategies

The changing of behavior alone creates a shift in thoughts and feelings and is an essential part of intervening with anger. This section offers a variety of behavioral techniques that will aid clients in addressing their anger. As they work to create behavioral changes, it is important to reinforce the letting go of old behaviors and the creation of new ones. Practicing new behaviors repeatedly is vital as repetition is the key to change.

Words challenges clients to address how respect is demonstrated. Rather than approaching life from a defensive and reactive stance they are encouraged to be proactive in seeking and articulating positive thoughts and feelings. The session Experience of Pleasurable Feelings in the Affective Strategies section is a good complement to this session.

Fair Fighting offers a constructive model of discussion when there is disagreement and gives a structured format to follow at times of high risk for inappropriate behavior.

Anger Callouts presents specific problem solving strategies that move clients from a feeling of anger to a healthy behavioral response.

Stress Reduction offers a variety of stress reducing techniques. By practicing specific behavioral techniques clients will be able to reduce negative thinking and respond more constructively to stressful stimuli and situations.

Nutrition explores dietary habits with clients and their use of sugar, caffeine and tobacco. People with anger issues seldom have healthy eating habits and typically eat foods that stimulate agitated behavior or mask feelings they are attempting to avoid or deny. This session will aid them in choosing healthier foods and eating patterns.

Outside Influences offers an opportunity to recognize how reading materials, music, television, and videos can shape one's thinking, either being supportive or unsupportive of treatment goals.

Triggers is a critical session to help clients be accountable for their own well being by identifying specific memories, situations, and/or people that trigger anger responses. Knowing one's triggers and having a plan of action provides clients the opportunity to be proactive in recovery.

Words

Objectives

To articulate caring feelings.
To identify respectful behaviors

Materials Needed

Handout – Words
Handout – Respecting Others

Starting Point

Angry people use their voices like fists. They beat up people with words. They have forgotten or never knew how to verbalize pleasantries or caring thoughts such as saying please, thank you, or I love you.

Give clients the handout Words and, as they complete it, discuss how they feel as they acknowledge their thoughts and feelings about the people in their lives. It is very possible that some of them will be unable to identify ways in which they tell or show someone that they love or care for them, or if they can it's only out of guilt after an act of their inappropriate anger. Discuss appropriate ways to express and share loving, caring feelings.

For someone who is chronically angry, this exploration can also lead into discussing the necessity of showing love rather than just speaking the words. Actions speak louder than words to those who have been on the receiving end of someone's anger. Talk about showing love without expectations; loving behavior is in the doing.

To an angry person, the use of *please* and *thank you* may imply vulnerability, a recognition that someone has something they want and that it could set them up for rejection. Ask clients to identify situations in which they didn't respond with respect or politeness and then discuss what the experience might have been like if they had used the words "please" and "thank you." Discuss other words that we use in different circumstances such as, excuse me, would you mind, I would prefer, etc.

Offer clients the handout Respecting Others as a resource to refer to in their daily lives.

Words

Make a list of significant persons in your life. Under each person's name, note as many qualities or behaviors that you like/value about that person. Then note the ways in which you show/tell this person that you love or care about them.

Name: _____

What I like/value about this person is:

_____

_____

I show/tell this person I love/care about him/her by:

_____

_____

Name: _____

What I like/value about this person is:

_____

_____

I show/tell this person I love/care about him/her by:

_____

_____

Name: _____

What I like/value about this person is:

_____

_____

I show/tell this person I love/care about him/her by:

_____

_____

Name: _____

What I like/value about this person is:

_____

_____

I show/tell this person I love/care about him/her by:

_____

_____

Name: _____

What I like/value about this person is:

_____

_____

I show/tell this person I love/care about him/her by:

_____

_____

_____

Name: _____

What I like/value about this person is:

_____

_____

I show/tell this person I love/care about him/her by:

_____

_____

Name: _____

What I like/value about this person is:

_____

_____

I show/tell this person I love/care about him/her by:

_____

_____

Name: _____

What I like/value about this person is:

_____

_____

I show/tell this person I love/care about him/her by:

_____

_____

Respecting Others

Do

DO — Start each day with a promise to respect others

DO — Give praise out loud for the good you see in others

DO — Listen carefully to what others say

DO — Look for things to appreciate in others

DO — Tell others they are worthwhile and important to you

DO — Tell others they are good and lovable

DO — Let others take responsibility for their lives while taking responsibility for yours

DO — Sit down, talk quietly and speak in a calm voice even when you disagree

DO — Pass up chances to insult, attack, or criticize

Don't

DON'T — Look for things to criticize

DON'T — Make fun of or laugh at others or call others names

DON'T — Make faces, roll your eyes, or sneer

DON'T — Insult others or put people down in front of others

DON'T — Ignore others or act superior

DON'T — Say others don't belong, or you wish they were dead

DON'T — Tell others how to run their lives

DON'T — Tell others they're weird or crazy

DON'T — Say others are not good enough, or unlovable

Fair Fighting

Objective

To develop conflict resolution skills.

Materials Needed

Handout – Fair Fighting Rules

Starting Point

Angry persons may ask for what they want, but if they don't get it, they may try persuasion or manipulation. If that doesn't work they may make threats and if that still doesn't work, they may attack. Give clients the handout Fair Fighting Rules. Then offer the following thoughts.

Didactic

No two people agree on everything. This means that some conflict is normal. How can you handle disagreements without going back to your old angry ways?

Anger is a messenger that lets you know something is wrong. Anger gives you the energy to do something about it, but it is only a messenger, not a solution. Anger doesn't fix anything. To resolve anger you need to ask for what you want, not whine or grumble or demand or threaten. That means knowing what you want and how to sort out the important from the unimportant. It means being direct, specific, and polite. State what is bothering you, what you want, and the reason for what you want. Be willing to negotiate and compromise.

Follow these fair fighting rules and you'll be more apt to be heard and hear others:

Do

Tell people what you want

Stick to one issue at a time

Sit down to talk

Listen

Focus on the specific behavior you want

Make regular eye contact (don't glare)

Be flexible, willing to change your mind

Breathe calmly, stay relaxed

Don't

Make fun of others or name call

Hit, push, shove, hold, or threaten to do so

Stand up and yell

Make faces

Attack the other's personality

Run away from the issue

Interrupt

Say anything that ignores the other's concerns, such as "forget it" or "I don't care"

Do	**Don't**
Be open to negotiation and compromise	Say "always" or "never" or other generalizations
Be responsible for everything you say	Insist on getting the last word in
Focus on solutions, not victories or defeats	Keep score
Set boundaries	
Take time-outs as needed	

After clients have reviewed the handout ask them to circle the items on the Don't list that are hardest for them, and circle the items on the Do list that they most need to follow. Ask them to share and then encourage them to practice, practice, practice.

Remind them to do four things when they make an anger mistake:

1. Admit it to themselves
2. Admit it to the appropriate people
3. Apologize and make whatever behavioral amends are possible
4. Commit to changing that behavior so as not to make the same mistake again

Fair Fighting Rules

Do	Don't
Tell people what you want	Make fun of others or name call
Stick to one issue at a time	Hit, push, shove, hold, or threaten to do so
Sit down to talk	Stand up and yell
Listen	Make faces
Focus on the specific behavior you want	Attack the other's personality
Make regular eye contact (don't glare)	Run away from the issue
Be flexible, willing to change your mind	Interrupt
Breathe calmly, stay relaxed	Say anything that discounts the other's concerns, such as "forget it" or "I don't care"
Be open to negotiation and compromise	Say "always' or "never" or other generalizations
Agree to disagree	Insist on getting the last word in
Be responsible for everything you say	Keep score
Focus on solutions, not victories or defeats	
Set boundaries	
Take time-outs as needed	

Circle the items on the **Don't** list that are hardest for you. Circle the items on the **Do** list that you most need to follow. Then practice, practice, practice.

If you lose your temper, go back to this list. You'll almost certainly find you broke a few Don'ts, or you forgot a few Do's.

You need to do four things when you make an anger mistake.

1. Admit it to yourself
2. Admit it to the appropriate people
3. Apologize and make whatever behavioral amends are possible
4. Commit to changing that behavior so you don't make the same mistake again

Anger Callouts

Objective

To learn effective responses to experiencing anger.

Materials Needed

Handout – Anger Callouts
Board

Starting Point

This session offers a visual picture to assessing and problem solving an angry situation. Ask clients to identify two situations in which they last became angry. Write them on a board and then use the handout Anger Callouts for discussion.

Offer the following examples to initially describe the use of the handout.

Example:
Another driver cuts me off on my way to work and I am infuriated.

Is the matter worth my continued attention? No.

Reason with yourself to cut anger short and challenge distorted thinking.
"He didn't see me." "I am nervous about my meeting at work today and I am overreacting."

Example:
I am angry at my 17 year old for wrecking my car.

Am I justified? Yes.

Do I have an effective response? No. "I want to say, you stupid so-and-so, I can't trust you with anything." Reason with yourself. Recognize distorted thinking.

Response is: "I wrecked my dad's car when I was fourteen. He didn't even take time to drive with me. Maybe I need to take more time with my son in the car for the sake of spending time with him, as well as teaching him driving skills."

Are you still angry? "Not so much. I can take reasonable action."

Continue this discussion using the examples clients initially identified. Walk clients through their situations to either assist them in developing an effective response or to identify behaviors that allow them to let go of their anger.

Anger Callouts
My angry feelings

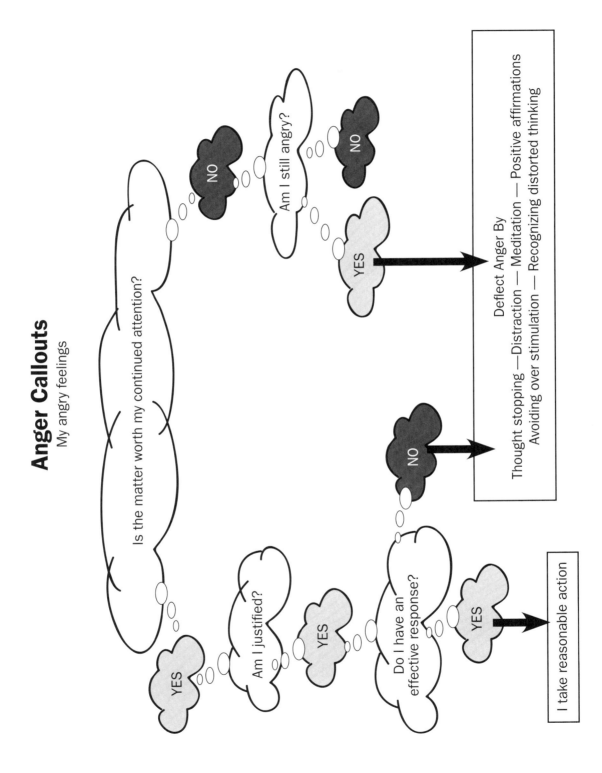

Is the matter worth my continued attention?

NO

Am I still angry?

NO

YES

Deflect Anger By

Thought stopping — Distraction — Meditation — Positive affirmations
Avoiding over stimulation — Recognizing distorted thinking

NO

YES

Am I justified?

YES

Do I have an effective response?

YES

I take reasonable action

Stress Reduction

Objectives

To practice relaxation techniques.
To reduce internal stress.

Materials Needed

Handout – Progressive Muscle Relaxation
CD Player
Imageries CD

Starting Point

Stress reduction exercises are vital in assisting the angry client, yet the timing of the exercises is very significant. These are people who are seen to be out of control while much of their life is spent in pent-up control. To do a full-scale relaxation exercise can be very frightening to them. In fact, it may be one of the most frightening aspects of their treatment experience. The concept of stress reduction and relaxation techniques must be introduced slowly. The following didactic would be a good place to begin.

Didactic

Chronically angry people often blame others for their stress. Whether or not you are blatantly angry or you repress anger, both types of people tend to have difficulty being aware of internal cues and signals. It is important to become more aware of the conditions inside one's own skin instead of staying exclusively externally focused.

Stored in your unconscious is a vast number of automatic programs without which you could not function normally. These programs are wired in at birth — in computer language: a part of your hardware. One of these programs tells your heart to beat so many beats per minute, another regulates blood pressure so you don't stroke out, and another regulates body temperature. You don't have to consciously think about these functions.

There are other programs, not programmed into the brain at birth, but acquired as a consequence of a process of repetition over time. After enough repetition, these learned programs become permanently etched into the subconscious.

An example of a learned program is driving.
You learn to drive a car from someone who already knows how. In the beginning it seems an overwhelming set of complex skills. The first time you get behind the wheel there is so much to remember. With practice, your skills markedly improve and much of the process becomes etched in your subconscious. After a year or two, driving becomes almost fully automatic to you. You no longer have to consciously think about stopping, turning, using the signals, applying the brakes. Putting the key into the ignition is the trigger that sets off the driving program within your brain.

Anger patterns are learned in much the same way.

Meditation, breathing, progressive relaxation, music, or imagery drive cynical thoughts from your mind and provide a calming effect. Your breathing and heart rate slow down. Blood pressure is lowered or stabilized. Stress hormone levels in your blood actually fall. Brain waves switch to a low arousal pattern as can be measured by an electroencephalogram. In some respects practicing meditation is like taking a fast-acting tranquilizer right then and there. By soothing biological fight or flight responses these techniques can help reduce the wear and tear that anger imposes on your heart, arteries, and immune system.

Share the following stress reduction techniques:

Deep Breathing

Ask clients to take a deep breath in, and slowly let the air out, then to repeat that slowly several times. Model this by doing the exercise as you instruct. Remind them to uncross their legs and arms. Again repeat the breathing. The message here is that the deeper the breathing, often the more honest one can be with oneself. With deeper breathing they are not attempting to go into a defensive stance.

Discuss the relevance of also needing to check breathing at various times in the day just to touch base with oneself. Explain how as a fast food, fast solution society we don't take time out in the course of the day to register our wants and feelings and then we often end up overreacting to a situation.

Encourage clients to pick a few times each day to simply stop and repeat the breathing exercise. When done, ask themselves, "What do I need right now?" "Do I need to take time to eat?" "Do I need to use the restroom?" "Do I need to go in and ask my co-worker something I am worried about versus assuming I know what she meant?" "What am I feeling?" "What is underneath that feeling?" "Where has this come from?" "What do I need to do with this?" So often needs are about basic self-care.

Relaxing Sigh

A sigh is often preceded by the sense that things are not quite as they should be, and by a feeling of tension. Because sighing releases some of that tension, it can be used at any time as a means of relaxing.

Ask clients to:

1. Sit or stand up straight.
2. Sigh deeply, letting out a sound of deep relief as the air rushes out of the lungs.
3. Just let the breath come in naturally — don't think about inhaling.
4. Repeat this procedure 8 to 12 times and experience the feeling of relaxation it provides.

Attitude Change

When feeling any form of anger:

- Sit down – don't stand
- Speak softly
- Don't swear
- Breathe evenly
- Talk slowly
- Don't exaggerate
- Listen

Listening to Music

Music can reduce anxiety and lessen irritability. The type of music — sounds of a running stream, the ocean, a waterfall, nature sounds — has been used as a means to relieve stress and lower anxiety and agitation. Soft music with soothing sounds, used alone or with relaxation techniques, is effective in helping to relax muscles and evoke a positive state of mind. Research suggests that these types of sounds promote the production of endorphins which are the body's own painkillers.

Progressive Muscle Relaxation

A more extensive stress reduction exercise is a progressive muscle relaxation. See Handout Progressive Muscle Relaxation. There are ways in which to lessen its full impact such as keeping clients in chairs, with lights on, and eyes open.

Adding music influences the experience in that it can make clients feel more vulnerable which they may interpret as being out of control and therefore they may react negatively. Again, the timing is important. Gauge how pent-up your clients are. Progressive muscle relaxation exercise is more likely to create less vulnerability than some types of visualization or imagery. Remember, for the angry person relaxing is about letting go of control. You need to pace clients and do it in a manner that is most safe for them.

After they complete a relaxation exercise, have clients discuss their experiences.

The **Imageries CD** has a *Relaxation Exercise* and *Letting Go Imagery*, both approximately eight minutes long that would be appropriate.

Ask clients to identify opportunities that come up in the day when they could do a mini-relaxation exercise on their own. Have them identify situations when they could do upper body letting go, arm relaxation, or leg relaxation. The goal is to incorporate this into their daily life.

Progressive Muscle Relaxation

Progressive muscle relaxation involves tensing and relaxing, in succession, the different muscle groups of the body. The idea is to tense each muscle group hard for about 10 seconds and then to let go of it suddenly. Then give yourself 15 - 20 seconds to relax, noticing how the muscle groups feel when relaxed in contrast to how they felt when tensed before you go on to the next group of muscles.

You may want to say to yourself, "I am relaxing, letting go," or any other relaxing phrase during each relaxation period between successive muscle groups. Throughout the exercise, maintain your focus on your muscles. If your attention wanders, bring it back to the particular muscle group you are working on.

Find a quiet location to practice and assume a comfortable position. Your entire body, including the head, should be supported. Lying down on a sofa or bed or sitting in a reclining chair are ways to support your body most completely. When lying down, a pillow beneath your knees offers further support. Sitting up is preferable to lying down if you're feeling tired and sleepy. Loosen or remove any tight clothing; take off your shoes, watch, glasses, contact lenses, jewelry and so on.

Give yourself permission to put aside the concerns of the day. Make a decision not to worry about anything.

Once you are comfortable, follow the detailed instructions:

1. To begin, take three deep abdominal breaths, exhaling slowly each time. As you exhale, imagine the tension throughout your body begins to flow away.

2. Clench your fists. Hold for 7 - 10 seconds, then release for 15 - 30 seconds. Use these same time intervals for all other muscle groups.

3. Tighten your biceps by drawing your forearms up toward your shoulders and "make a muscle" with both arms. Hold and then relax.

4. Tighten the triceps, the muscles on the undersides of your upper arms, by extending your arms out straight and locking your elbows. Hold and then relax.

5. Tense the muscles in your forehead by raising your eyebrows as far as you can. Hold... and then relax. Imagine your forehead muscles becoming smooth and limp as they relax.

6. Tense the muscles around your eyes by clenching your eyelids tightly shut. Hold and then relax. Imagine the sensation of deep relaxation spreading all around the area of your eyes.

7. Tighten your jaws by opening your mouth so wide that you stretch the muscles around the hinges of your jaw. Hold and then relax. Let your lips part and allow your jaw to hang loose.

8. Tighten the muscles in the back of your neck by dropping your head back as if you were going to touch your head to your back being gentle to avoid injury. Focus only on tensing the muscles in your neck. Hold and then relax.

9. Take a few deep breaths and focus on the weight of your head sinking into whatever it is resting on.

10. Raise your shoulders as if you were going to touch your ears. Hold and then relax.

11. Tighten the muscles around your shoulder blades by pushing your shoulder blades back as if you were going to touch them together. Hold the tension in your shoulder blades and then relax.

12. Tighten the muscles of your chest by taking in a deep breath. Hold for up to 10 seconds, and then release slowly. Imagine any excess tension in your chest flowing away with the exhalation.

13. Tighten your abdominal muscles by sucking in your abdomen. Hold and then release.

14. Tighten your lower back by arching it up. (Omit this step if you have lower back pain.) Hold and then relax.

15. Tighten your buttocks by pulling them together. Hold and then relax. Imagine muscles in your hips going loose and limp.

16. Squeeze the muscles in your thighs all the way down to your knees. Hold and then relax.

17. Tighten your calf muscles by pulling your toes toward you. Hold and then relax.

18. Tighten your feet by curling your toes downward. Hold and then relax.

19. Mentally scan your body for any residual tension. If a particular area remains tense, repeat one or two cycles for that group of muscles.

20. Now imagine a wave of relaxation spreading throughout your body, starting at your head and gradually penetrating every muscle group all the way down to your toes.

Nutrition

Objectives

To recognize the interplay of caffeine, sugar, and nicotine with angry feelings.
To identify and reinforce healthy eating patterns.

Materials Needed

Handout – Three Nutritional Demons
Handout – Dietary Discussion Questions
Handout – Basic Food Pyramid

Starting Point

Eating healthy is crucial for physical and mental health. People with anger problems seldom have healthy eating habits. They may skip meals, consume large amounts of sugars and starches, and are likely to smoke, drink alcoholic and/or caffeinated drinks, and use drugs.

Didactic

While it is common knowledge that nicotine, sugar and caffeine are extremely harmful to peoples' physical health, they are also major contributors to the excitement of anger. Caffeine, sugar, and nicotine are toxic stimulants that speed up the nervous and cardiovascular systems which in turn accelerates the fight or flight response that is already being accelerated with feelings of anger.

Some people will claim that nicotine, caffeine and sugar actually calm rather than stimulate them. In reality these substances can both invigorate and relax someone. This is called a biphasic effect, where there is a response, and then later another. Initially you feel a sense of calm but your body system is actually being stimulated which only helps to aggravate any feelings of anger.

Explore with clients their use of caffeine, sugar and nicotine. Nicotine use is easily recognized with the habit of smoking cigarettes or chewing tobacco. Caffeine is found in sodas, teas, coffee, chocolate, and a host of other foods. Primary sugars are found in candies, pies, cakes, ice creams, juice, sodas, and most processed foods. It is surprising the amount of sugar found in processed foods in the form of corn syrup and fructose. The amount of sugar and caffeine consumption is significant because both can contribute to mood changes that exacerbate low mood and agitation and, therefore, both should be avoided as much as possible.

The handout Three Nutritional Demons may be used to further this discussion.

The handout Dietary Discussion Questions gives clients the opportunity to consider their eating habits and use of substances.

Questions for discussion:

What do you eat for breakfast? When and where do you eat it?

What do you eat for lunch? When and where do you eat it?

What do you eat for dinner? When and where do you eat it?

Do you eat after 8 p.m. and if so, what do you eat?

How much water do you drink during the day?

What is your daily intake of caffeine (coffee, chocolate, sodas)?

How much sugar do you consume daily?

Do you read food labels?

Do you use alcohol and/or other drugs? If so, describe the extent of your use.

Do you smoke or chew tobacco? If so, describe the extent of your use.

What do you believe you need to consume more or less of to have a healthy diet?

Clients' responses to these questions may lead to more in-depth discussion about nutrition and can be expanded on greatly by addressing what they need to consume less of or stop, and what they need to incorporate into their eating patterns.

Continue by discussing the Basic Food Pyramid of bread, cereal, rice and pasta — vegetables and fruits — milk, yogurt, and cheese — meat, poultry, fish, dry beans, eggs and nuts — fats, oils and sweets. Reading product labels is helpful before choosing processed and canned foods that often contain sugar (corn syrup, fructose), and usually caffeine is present in sodas and all foods with chocolate. Depending on the depth of exploration desired, education about reading food labels to find hidden sugars and other stimulants could be helpful. It is likely that reading the ingredients of processed foods is not something clients have been doing. Making a grocery list and shopping when one is not hungry are helpful strategies to healthier eating.

Examine the behaviors that support unhealthy nutrition. If someone doesn't get out of bed until noon, one may rationalize eating a huge meal to satisfy the need for both breakfast and lunch. If they aren't willing to walk four blocks to a supermarket rather than one block to a convenience store, they are more likely to purchase processed foods instead of fruits, vegetables, dairy products, meat and fish.

Assist clients in identifying behaviors that support healthier nutrition. Some simple yet significant suggestions are to increase the amount of water one drinks; switch to decaffeinated coffee, herbal teas or decaffeinated sodas; and replace sugar with sugar substitutes, sugarless sweets, fresh or dried fruits, and fresh vegetables. Most markets have a wide variety of fresh and packaged food that is low in sugars or sugarless. Recognizing that caffeine, sugar, and nicotine are sought in an attempt to calm oneself, direct clients to other means of relaxation such as exercise, yoga, meditation, listening to music, etc.

Have clients identify a dietary goal for the next week. Keep the goal realistic and simple such as eating one fruit serving at breakfast each day, or eating one vegetable serving at lunch or dinner each day, or eating breakfast no later than 9 a.m., reducing caffeine intake, or reading food labels. Continue with weekly reports and support and, as clients are ready, increase goals.

Three Nutritional Demons

1. Do you smoke or chew tobacco? Would you like to reduce or give up your use of nicotine?

   If you smoke or chew tobacco describe how you may use nicotine in relationship to feeling anger.

2. In what foods or drinks do you consume caffeine? I.e. coffee, tea, soda, chocolate, other.

   Describe how you may use caffeine in relationship to feeling anger.

3. How much sugar is in your diet?

   Describe your intake of processed carbohydrates, sweets, sugared sodas, sugar in coffee, etc.

   Describe how you may use sugar in relationship to feeling angry.

Dietary Discussion Questions

1. What do you eat for breakfast? When and where do you eat it?

2. What do you eat for lunch? When and where do you eat it?

3. What do you eat for dinner? When and where do you eat it?

4. Do you eat after 8 p.m. and if so, what do you eat?

5. How much water do you drink during the day?

6. What is your daily intake of caffeine (coffee, chocolate, sodas)?

7. How much sugar do you consume daily?

8. Do you read food labels?

9. Do you use alcohol and/or other drugs? If so, describe the extent of your use.

10. Do you smoke or chew tobacco? If so describe the extent of your use.

11. What do you believe you need to consume more or less of to have a healthy diet?

Basic Food Pyramid

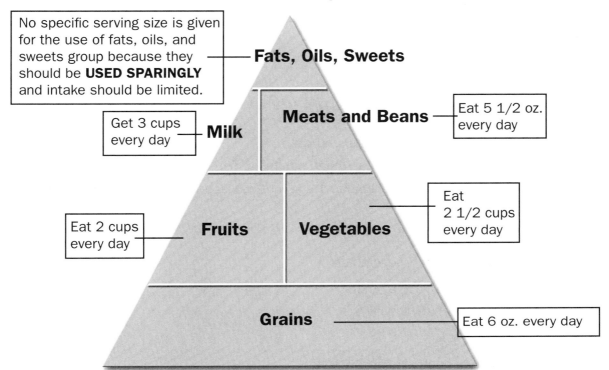

No specific serving size is given for the use of fats, oils, and sweets group because they should be **USED SPARINGLY** and intake should be limited.

Fats, Oils, Sweets

Meats and Beans — Eat 5 1/2 oz. every day

Get 3 cups every day — **Milk**

Fruits — Eat 2 cups every day

Vegetables — Eat 2 1/2 cups every day

Grains — Eat 6 oz. every day

Grains	Vegetables	Fruits	Milk	Meat & Beans
Make half your grains whole grains Eat at least 3 oz. of whole-grain cereals, breads, crackers, rice, or pasta every day 1oz. is about 1 slice of bread, about 1 cup of cereal, or 1/2 cup of cooked rice, cereal or pasta	Vary your veggies Eat more dark-green veggies like broccoli, spinach, and other dark, leafy greens. Eat more orange vegetables like carrots and sweet potatoes	Focus on fruits Eat a variety of fruit Choose fresh, frozen, canned, or dried fruit	Get your calcium rich foods Go low-fat or fat-free when you choose milk, yogurt, and other milk products If you don't or can't consume milk, choose lactose-free products or other calcium sources such as fortified foods and beverages	Go lean with protein Choose low-fat or lean meats and poultry Bake it, broil it, or grill it Vary your protein routine – choose more fish, beans, peas, nuts, and seeds

What counts as a serving size?

Listed below are the approximate amounts that count as one serving.

Milk, Yogurt, and Cheese

- 1 cup of milk or yogurt
- 1 1/2 ounces of natural cheese
- 2 ounces of processed cheese

Meat, Poultry, Fish, Dry Beans, Eggs, and Nuts

- 2-3 ounces of cooked lean meat, poultry, or fish
- 1/2 cup of cooked dry beans, 1 egg, or 2 tablespoons of peanut butter count as 1 ounce of lean meat

Vegetables

- 1 cup of raw leafy vegetables
- 1/2 cup of other vegetables cooked or chopped raw
- 3/4 cup of vegetable juice

Fruits

- 1 medium apple, banana, orange
- 1/2 cup of chopped, cooked, or canned fruit
- 3/4 cup of fruit juice

Bread, Cereal, Rice, and Pasta

- 1 slice of bread
- 1 ounce of ready-to-eat cereal
- 1/2 cup of cooked cereal, rice, or pasta

Try to meet all the recommended serving size amounts listed above. Your body needs them for the vitamins, minerals, carbohydrates, and protein they supply.

Remember, the Food Pyramid is not a rigid prescription, but a valuable reference to help you eat healthy and increase the quality of your life.

Adapted from a model at www.mypyramid.gov

Outside Influences

Objective

To identify whether or not outside influences support healthy and calm behaviors.

Materials Needed

Handout – Outside Influences

Starting Point

It is important for clients to be conscious of the influences that shape their thinking. The handout Outside Influences offers questions for consideration and discussion.

As you explore these questions with clients, include a discussion about when it is that they engage in the behavior. Do they watch television news prior to going to bed? Would they sleep better by listening to soothing music or a meditation recording? Do they read books with tension-filled stories of violence or unrest? If so, how would they go about choosing books that would entertain but do not provoke stress?

There are many people in clients' lives such as co-workers and extended family with whom they do not have total choice of the involvement. As clients respond to question number four on the handout ask them to be very specific with their responses. If a client is in need of more involvement with supportive people, you may need to problem-solve how to increase such interaction.

Outside Influences

Questions for consideration and discussion:
(Circle the words that best describe your answer)

1. How would you describe the music you listen to?

    loud   violent lyrics   sad   soothing   relaxing   energizing   other _____

    Is this music supportive or unsupportive of your healing and recovery process?
    Supportive   Unsupportive
    Describe

2. How would you describe the videos, movies, or TV shows you watch?

    violent   tension-filled   frightening   funny   uplifting   inspiring   dark

    explicit   escapist   other _____

    Are these programs supportive or unsupportive of your healing and recovery process?
    Supportive   Unsupportive
    Describe

3. How would you describe the books or magazines you read?

    educational   inspirational   humorous   violent   fantasy   romantic   informative
    other _____

    Are these materials supportive or unsupportive of your healing and recovery process?
    Supportive   Unsupportive
    Describe

4. How would you describe the people you allow in your life?

    intrusive   loud   negative   hurtful   shaming   respectful   caring   loving

    playful   kind   needy   patient   accepting   demanding   generous

    other _____

    Are they supportive or unsupportive of your healing and recovery process?
    Supportive   Unsupportive
    Describe

Triggers

Objective

To identify potential anger triggers and develop appropriate plan of intervention.

Materials Needed

Handout – Triggers

Starting Point

On a daily basis clients will encounter experiences — triggers — that heighten the risk of unhealthy anger. While not all triggers can be avoided, people can learn what to do when they find themselves in a vulnerable situation.

Didactic

Triggers are specific memories, situations, and behaviors that jeopardize recovery from the unhealthy expression of anger. Pulling the trigger on a gun signals that a bullet is being fired. For people coping with anger issues, triggers may lead the way to a downward spiral of hopelessness, despair, and acting out behaviors.

Jonathan describes triggers. "It's been a year since I last saw Katie, but I still drive by her old apartment sometimes. Every time I do, I get a knot in the pit of my stomach. I envision her with someone else, laughing, touching, and it makes me jealous. I become enraged and head to a local bar and invariably pick a fight with someone."

For Jonathan, a significant trigger to his anger is environmental; the sight of his former girlfriend's apartment. His distorted thinking leads him to believe that he'll feel better after driving by Katie's old place, but instead he feels worse, becoming agitated and angry.

Carl describes triggers to his anger this way. "I was out at a restaurant with friends having an okay time when they played a song about being in love. My friends were all talking about their wives and kids and I don't even have a girlfriend. No matter how I tried, I couldn't stop thinking about how things never seem to work out for me. After listening to their stories for twenty minutes, I told my friends I had to leave. I drove off in my car feeling really angry, got pulled over for speeding, talked back to the cop and was nearly arrested."

Carl's trigger is social and situational. It occurs spontaneously as a result of ordinary activity. His distorted thinking leads him to believe that his situation will never change. He feels a sense of hopelessness that he quickly converts into anger.

Kathleen's triggers are young beautiful women. After thirty years of marriage, her husband divorced her and married a 25-year-old woman. He was having affairs with women considerably younger throughout their marriage. Hence, being around young women quickly fuels Kathleen's negative thinking patterns.

Triggers can be nearly anything ranging from places — certain rooms in a house, a specific restaurant — to something such as a movie, the computer, a picture, to a situation: a wedding, office gathering, or holiday ritual.

Ask clients to complete the handout Triggers, and then discuss it.

Triggers

Identify significant triggers that you are aware of.

1)_____

2)_____

3)_____

In what situations do you feel most triggered?

1)_____

2)_____

3)_____

Identify healthy cognitions (thoughts) that will help you to cope with your most significant triggers.

1)_____

2)_____

3)_____

Identify behaviors that will help you practice self-care and/or de-escalate the situation when faced with your most significant triggers.

1)_____

2)_____

3)_____

Addiction Strategies

Overview of
Addiction Strategies

While this section is presented in the mid portion of this book, it is not meant to imply that it should only be considered midway into the treatment process. Because the use of alcohol and other drugs influences anger, the session Alcohol, Drugs and Anger may be explored early in the process. Relapse Connection and Incorporation of the Use of Steps are most applicable to clients in recovery from addictive disorders. Many people in recovery, whether recovery is from a substance or behavior, maintain the expression of unhealthy anger and are in great need of therapy to help them address their anger issues. Whether or not a client has other addictions, it is common that his or her relationship with anger is highly addictive and there is much to be gained by working with anger from an addictive model. Facilitator should become familiar with all of these sessions and incorporate them as is appropriate.

Alcohol, Drugs, and Anger is essential in working with anyone with anger problems. Due to the strong correlation between the inappropriate expression of anger and the use of alcohol and/or other drugs, it is vital to recognize the possibility of how substances fuel anger problems.

Addictive Anger explores the possibility of anger as an addiction similar to other addictive disorders. A questionnaire, adapted from the addictions field for anger-related issues, is offered as an assessment tool.

Relapse Connection is an important session for clients in recovery from other addictions because anger is a significant contributor to relapse. While this entire book offers a form of relapse prevention it is helpful to specifically address how anger contributes to relapse.

Incorporation of the Use of Steps is a very effective model of recovery particularly for clients who already use a Twelve Step program for recovery. This is a model they already trust and can easily adopt.

Alcohol, Drugs, and Anger

Objective

To recognize the connection between alcohol and/or other drug usage and the expression of anger.

Materials Needed

Handout – Substances and Anger

Starting Point

Ask clients to complete the handout Substances and Anger. Then discuss whether or not clients see any connection between their use of alcohol and/or other drugs and their anger/aggression. This obviously leads to discussion about the ability to stop using or drinking and using available adjunct resources.

Studies indicate that anger and substance abuse are two problems that are practically twins. More than half the people in treatment for alcohol and/or drug addiction(s) have major anger problems. This manifests itself with people in recovery too; people who stay clean but are on a dry drunk because they have ignored their anger problems. Some people will use alcohol or other drugs to avoid their anger and having to deal with their real issues. It may work for a time, but eventually their anger will explode.

Even if someone is not addicted, when under the influence of a substance he or she may use being loaded as an excuse for the escalation of anger. This is merely an excuse. Alcohol and drugs don't afford time out from reality. Everyone is responsible for what goes in one's own mouth, nose, or arm, and for everything one says or does with or without that substance.

Depending on your clients, you may deem it appropriate to further the discussion on chemical dependency and be open to referral for assessment.

Substances and Anger

The use of alcohol and/or drugs is frequently associated with anger and aggression.

Substance	Current or recent use?	Past use?	Frequency
Alcohol	Yes / No	Yes / No	_____
Amphetamines (Cocaine, Crystal Meth, Crack, Crank, diet pills)	Yes / No	Yes / No	_____
Cannabis (THC - marijuana, hashish)	Yes / No	Yes / No	_____
Anabolic Steroids	Yes / No	Yes / No	_____
Opiates (Heroin, Morphine, Oxycodone, Opium, RX pain pills)	Yes / No	Yes / No	_____
Inhalants (Ether, nitrous oxide, amyl nitrite, benzene, glue, aerosols, paint thinner)	Yes / No	Yes / No	_____
Hallucinogens (MDMA - Ecstasy, LSD, PCP, Peyote)	Yes / No	Yes / No	_____
Barbiturates (Phenobarbital, GHB- Gamma Butyrolactone, tranquilizers, hypnotic sedatives)	Yes / No	Yes / No	_____

Check those that relate to you:

_____ My anger/aggression gets worse when using.

_____ I only get in trouble with my anger/aggression while using.

_____ I'm less angry/aggressive when I drink or use drugs, or I act out in other compulsive ways, e.g. gambling, engaging in sex, working excessively, etc.

_____ Other people tell me there is a connection but I have trouble believing it.

_____ I see no connection at all.

_____ Other substance connections with anger/aggression (explain).

_____

_____

Alcohol, Drugs, and Anger

Addictive Anger

Objectives

To recognize the addictive nature of anger.
To identify the destructive consequences of anger behaviors.

Materials Needed

Handout – Twenty Anger Questions

Starting Point

Using the indicators of addictive disorders, this session will help clients to recognize how anger can be addictive.

Didactic

For many people struggling with anger problems their relationship with anger is as strong as an alcoholic's relationship with alcohol, a cocaine addict's relationship with cocaine, and a gambler's relationship with gambling. They see anger as the solution or answer to all situations which ultimately destroys every aspect of their lives. Yet the angry person seems incapable of reacting to life differently.

As with other addictions, in anger addiction there is . . .

- Build up of tolerance
- Loss of control
- Negative consequence
- Jekyll and Hyde personality
- Inability to stop the behavior

Anger comes to be the way some people define themselves when they find themselves addicted to the rush, the intensity, and sense of power and aliveness that anger produces. Like other addictions, its immediate consequences such as damaged relationships, lost jobs, decline in personal health, and peace of mind are certainly costly, but not unpleasant enough to cancel the pleasurable sense of power and control that the expression of anger accords the anger addict.

As anyone who has felt violent anger knows, there is tremendous power in anger. Enraged, you are likely to experience a heightened sense of being alive and alert, and of time moving in slow motion. This reaction is essentially biochemical. Anger triggers a rush of adrenaline (epinephrine) to the bloodstream and increases blood pressure, pulse rate, and respiration rate — the "flight or fight" syndrome, so named because presumably these physical changes once prepared our ancestors either to run or fight for their lives.

Everyone has experienced these feelings at one time or another. What distinguishes the anger addict is that he/she needs the rush of excitement that anger produces, and often looks for or sets up situations that will provide an excuse to explode. With some forms of the addiction long periods of calm will make the addict uneasy, feeling dull, depressed, and bored. Like anyone else with a physical dependence, the anger addict feels increasingly edgy and powerless the longer he/she goes without an anger "fix." Eventually, this edginess leads an addict to provoke a conflict to relieve the tension, or to blow up for entirely inappropriate reasons. In some cases, an addict may not wait for an excuse to explode, and instead maintain a state of continuous, simmering rage.

This dependence explains why anger is the addict's only response to stress. If an addict is consciously or unconsciously looking for a reason to explode, then any sort of conflict will produce an outburst. Anger addicts do not argue to persuade, they do not even argue to win. They argue to get the fix!

In the same manner, the compulsive repetition of anger as a reaction to problems in day-to-day life can lead to a self-perpetuating destructive pattern. It isn't necessarily the element i.e., drugs, alcohol, etc., to which an individual becomes addicted, but rather the compelling need to perform the function of the addiction repeatedly. Need becomes the key word, as well as the focus and motivation, for the activity. In this vein, need develops quickly into compulsive drive that is re-enacted again and again. The anger addict has learned through painful experience to rely on the "high" of this adrenaline rush to give a sense of power. This high is analogous to the one that runners report feeling through the release of endorphins on long distance runs. The anger addict is biochemically addicted to this self-produced drug. It makes him/her a force with which to be reckoned, rather than the scared and helpless child he/she was before the discovery of the singular response — *anger.*

Ask clients to recognize and discuss the similarities between chemical addiction and anger addiction. The handout Twenty Anger Questions may be used to further discussion.

As with recovery from other addictions, the anger addict has to give up living in extremes and seek moderation and balance. It is like trading in a familiar but worn out car that doesn't get you where you want to be for a new model. This new model gets you where you want to go and allows you to experience a range of normal feelings: peace of mind, a sense of calm, and healthy ways of relating. As hopeful as this change sounds, it may seem as awkward and challenging as speaking a newly learned foreign language; because it's unfamiliar it may be scary. As intimidating as new behaviors, thoughts, and feelings may be, the promises of recovery are ever present.

It's important to remember that recovery from distorted anger issues, like recovery from other addictions, doesn't occur in isolation. Recovery is about connection — connection with self and with others — and is most attainable when you allow others to be a part of the process.

Twenty Anger Questions

1. Yes No   Have you ever felt remorse after your angry behavior?
2. Yes No   Do you tend to make impulsive decisions when you feel angry?
3. Yes No   Does anger give you feelings of self-confidence and power?
4. Yes No   Does your anger make you careless of your family's welfare?
5. Yes No   Has your ambition decreased due to anger?
6. Yes No   Does anger cause you difficulty in sleeping?
7. Yes No   Have you ever had a loss of memory as a result of anger?
8. Yes No   Has a physician, therapist, or other professional ever treated you for anger?
9. Yes No   Do you find yourself drinking or using to dissipate angry feelings?
10. Yes No   Do you wake up in an angry mood for no apparent reason?
11. Yes No   Have you ever had a complete loss of control due to anger?
12. Yes No   Have you ever been arrested or hospitalized due to your anger?
13. Yes No   Have you ever had health problems caused by internalized stress (ulcers, migraine headaches, hives)?
14. Yes No   Does your anger make your homelife unhappy?
15. Yes No   Has anyone ever suggested that your anger is a problem?
16. Yes No   Has anger affected your reputation?
17. Yes No   Have you made promises to control your anger and then broken them?
18. Yes No   Have you ever gotten into financial, legal, or marital difficulties due to your anger?
19. Yes No   Have you ever lost time from work because of your anger?
20. Yes No   Have you ever felt guilt or shame about your anger?

If you answered Yes to any four of these questions, your anger may be a problem.

If you answered Yes to any five of these questions, your anger is a problem that warrants attention.

If you answered Yes to six or more of these questions, your anger is definitely a serious problem and you need to seek immediate therapeutic attention.

Adapted from a model of a chemical dependency questionnaire used by John Hopkins Hospital

Relapse Connection

Objective

To recognize the role of anger in relapse from addiction recovery.

Materials Needed

Handout – Relapse Connection
Paper and pens

Starting Point

Anger is a significant contributor to relapse in addictive disorders. Masking the reality of anger or being caught up in the rush of anger without being aware of what is occurring often leads one to relapse without warning. One needs to develop a respect for anger. The goal of anger recovery is not to ever be angry; it is to learn how to recognize anger, use it constructively, experience it, and then let it go.

To set the tone for discussing the relationship of anger to relapse from other addictions, particularly if clients are members of a Twelve Step program, the following quotes may be appreciated.

Didactic

It was Bill W., cofounder of Alcoholics Anonymous, who wrote, *"Resentment is the Number One offender. It destroys more alcoholics that anything else. From it stem all forms of spiritual disease, for we have been not only mentally and physically ill, we have also been spiritually ill. When our spiritual malady is overcome, we straighten out mentally and physically.*

In dealing with our resentments, we set them on paper. We listed people, institutions, or principles with whom we were angry. We asked ourselves why we were angry. In most cases it was found that our self-esteem, our pocketbooks, our ambitions, our personal relationships (including sex) were hurt or threatened. The most heated bit of letter writing can be a wonderful safety valve — providing the wastebasket is somewhere nearby."

He goes on to say —
"Few people have been more victimized by resentments than have we alcoholics. A burst of temper could spoil a day, and a well-nursed grudge could make us miserably ineffective. Nor were we ever skillful in separating justified from unjustified anger. As we saw it, our wrath was always justified. Anger, that occasional luxury of more balanced people, could keep us on an emotional jag indefinitely. These 'dry benders' often led straight to the bottle."
As Bill Sees It, The A.A. Way of Life. Selected Writings of A.A.'s Co-Founder Bill Wilson pages 39 and 179.

The handout Relapse Connection needs to be discussed extensively and can easily be presented in two sessions, part one and part two as divided in the handout. After years of utilizing this exercise, the author holds the strong belief that the addicted person knows what his or her relapse could look like. For the facilitator to think they don't know is professional denial. By encouraging clients to describe their relapse, it is taken apart step by step, with action steps created to prevent the possibility of it occurring.

Relapse Connection

Part One:
You may be in recovery from alcohol/drug or food addictions, or other compulsive behaviors. Check the connections between anger and your addiction that most apply to you:

- ☐ I use or act out because I want my anger to go away.
- ☐ I use or act out because I want to let my anger out.
- ☐ I use or act out to get back at other people when I am angry.
- ☐ I use or act out because when I am angry I don't care about anything or anyone.
- ☐ I use or act out in order to hurt or punish myself with my anger.
- ☐ Other

Give three examples from your past for each connection you checked above.

1. _____

2. _____

3. _____

Part Two:
List three situations that most commonly trigger your addiction and relate to your being or becoming angry.

1. _____

2. _____

3. _____

On a separate piece of paper, based on the above:

1. Write the story of your next relapse and predict how it might happen.

2. List the signals or warning signs you need to watch for in light of what you predicted.

3. List what you need to do to prevent a relapse if/when you notice these signals.

Incorporation of the Use of Steps

Objective

To utilize the philosophy of Twelve Step programs in anger recovery.

Materials Needed

Handout – Anger's Seven Steps
Handout – The Twelve Suggested Steps
Paper and pens

Starting Point

If any client is a member of a Twelve Step program, he or she will find value in applying the Twelve Steps of their program to address their anger. To enhance your understanding of the value of the suggested steps, or if facilitator is unfamiliar with these programs, it may be helpful to read the Twelve Steps and Twelve Traditions of Alcoholics Anonymous.

If the facilitator is incorporating the steps into the treatment process, begin with clients openly acknowledging the first step and sharing this within the group. It may be appropriate to only review the first step and tell clients that it is up to them to decide when they are ready to admit Step One and that they may do so at the beginning of any of the sessions. If any clients are steeped in Twelve Step recovery, the handouts Anger's Seven Steps and The Twelve Suggested Steps can be offered as resources for their own use outside of the therapy process.

Didactic

These anger seven steps are adapted from the Twelve Steps of Alcoholics Anonymous.

Anger Step One — Admit you are angry and your life has become problematic as a result of the destructive and unhealthy expression of anger.
It is uncomfortable for people to admit that their lives have become problematic as a result of their own behavior. Prior to recognizing that you are responsible for your own behavior you try everything possible to hold others responsible, believing there is no choice in the matter. Yet your life remains dominated by anger which escalates in its consequences. When you actually come to grips with yourself that you are angry, that your life is problematic as a result of your response to your anger, you are able to see the facts of your life in true perspective. The purpose here is not to judge yourself. It is your opportunity to observe your behavior and to admit you need help. When you see your behavior as it really is and are willing to be honest with yourself, you have taken the first step toward change and greater serenity.

Ask clients to write out Step One acknowledging the unmanageability of their lives as a consequence of their anger, and to admit that their anger is a problem.

Anger Step Two — Demonstrate a willingness to do something about your anger.
If it is your choice to be in a treatment process, that may in fact be demonstrating a willingness to do something about the problem. Your participation and willingness to take responsibility for your own actions constitutes recognition of this step.

Remind clients that they need to remain vigilant to Step Two everyday. Discuss ways in which they demonstrate willingness, or what they can do to reinforce remaining vigilant, i.e., affirmations, meditation, or prayer.

Anger Step Three — Take a personal inventory of how anger has affected your life.
Look squarely at the unhappiness your anger has caused others and yourself. These questions will assist you with your inventory:

- When, how, and in what instances did your anger damage other people and you?
- What people have been hurt and how badly?
- How has your anger hurt your relationship with your spouse or partner?
- How has it hurt your relationship with your children?
- How has anger hurt your relationships within your original family?
- How has anger influenced you at work, with getting a job, your career?
- How has it affected your financial security?
- How has anger hurt your relationships with friends?
- Have you used anger as an excuse for promiscuity outside of a committed monogamous relationship?
- Does anger influence your sexual behavior?

Anger Step Four — Using your personal inventory as a tool, admit to yourself, to your God, and to another human being, a friend, sponsor, therapist, minister, how it is you have been hurtful with your anger, hurtful not only to others but to yourself as well.
The tendency is to sweep your experiences away, to not remember. It is in admitting how your anger has been hurtful to yourself and others that you display the first tangible evidence of your willingness to move forward. Talking allows you to move out of denial and take responsibility for your behavior. This is very hard to do. You would prefer to keep much of your behavior secret, but it is in keeping it secret that you continue your old behaviors. Few people are able to let go of negative and hurtful behavior when they continue to deny the impact it has on others and where they maintain the shame-shrouded secrecy of their behavior.

Anger Step Five — Make a written list of those you have harmed. Include yourself, and be willing to make amends.
You cannot remake the present until you undo the past. List the people you have hurt with your anger and identify the things you have done that caused physical, emotional and/or spiritual harm to them. Be specific. Be aware the person you may have harmed the most

could be yourself. You may be your own worst enemy and your resentment against yourself manifests in the form of self-blame, guilt, and shame. Consider the following:

- With which people on your list do you feel the greatest need to make amends?
- What are your feelings toward the person you need to make amends with?
- Are you willing to go to any length to make the amends?
- Do you have any reluctance to make amends?

Anger Step Six — Make direct amends to such people whenever possible, except when to do so would injure them or others.

Amend-making is often accomplished in the form of a verbal or written apology, but it is just as significantly achieved in the change of behavior. Although you sincerely want to change your behavior and hope to behave differently than you have in the past, you often don't have the skill to do it differently. Amends making also includes making a commitment to yourself to be willing to put forth the effort to learn new skills.

When you make amends you do so as a part of your being accountable for your own behavior. This is not about changing your behavior so that others will like you better or be more loving towards you. Don't go into amends making with expectations about other people's behavior, but with an expectation that you need to do this for you solely.

Good judgment, a careful sense of timing, courage, and prudence are qualities that you will apply when taking this step. It is wise to reflect upon your intended amends for a while. Forethought will prepare you for appropriate timing and deter you from causing any further harm. When making amends, there are those people who are readily accessible and those with whom you will not be able to make direct personal contact. The latter involves people who are deceased or are no longer a part of your life. In these cases, an indirect amends can satisfy your need to make things right. You can make indirect amends through prayer or by writing a letter, as if you are actually communicating with the offended person. Another example of an indirect amends is making an anonymous donation to an organization or company that you stole money from.

Be careful not to confuse apologies with amends. Apologies are sometimes called for, but apologies are not amends. Amends are made by behaving differently. You can apologize a hundred times for being late for work, but this will not "mend" the tardiness. Appearing at work on time evinces a change in behavior, and thus becomes an amends.

A discussion about staying focused on the purpose of amends needs to be reinforced so that clients don't get inappropriately preoccupied on how their amends is received.

Anger Step Seven — Continue to take a personal inventory of whether or not you are angry and when you are, promptly admit it.

Take a few minutes every day to touch base with yourself to allow the opportunity for self-honesty. Are you angry because you feel threatened and are being defensive? Are you masking your anger with other emotions such as sadness or fear? Are you swallowing your anger because you are frightened of other people's disapproval?

Your commitment to continue working the Anger Steps is acknowledgment of your intention to improve the quality of your life and your relationships.

Several other of the steps listed in the handout The Twelve Suggested Steps are as important as those that have been incorporated into the Anger Seven Steps.

- Came to believe that a Power greater than ourselves could restore us to sanity.
- Made a decision to turn our will and our lives over to the care of God, *as we understood Him.*
- Admitted to God, to ourselves and to another human being the exact nature of our wrongs.
- Were entirely ready to have God remove all these defects of character.
- Humbly asked Him to remove our shortcomings.
- Sought through prayer and meditation to improve our conscious contact with God, *as we understood Him,* praying only for knowledge of His will for us, and the power to carry that out.

The subsequent section, Spirituality Strategies, assists clients in exploring the role of a "power greater than themselves" in their recovery process.

Another practice of Twelve Step programs is that of engaging a sponsor. Sponsorship is a peer based self-help model. A sponsor is typically someone in recovery from the same issues who acts as mentor and assists and possibly directs another person in his or her recovery process. For a person who is struggling with anger issues, a sponsor is someone who has also battled anger and is actively and behaviorally demonstrating recovery. If any of your clients are active members of a Twelve Step program and have partnered with a sponsor, they will very likely recognize this resource as a means to assist them with their anger recovery.

Anger's Seven Steps

Step One
Admit you are angry and your life has become problematic as a result of the destructive and unhealthy expression of anger.

Step Two
Demonstrate a willingness to do something about your anger.

Step Three
Take a personal inventory of how anger has affected your life.

Step Four
Using your personal inventory as a tool, admit to yourself, to your God, and to another human being, a friend (sponsor, therapist, minister) how it is you have been hurtful with your anger, hurtful not only to others but to yourself as well.

Step Five
Make a written list of those you have harmed. Include yourself, and be willing to make amends.

Step Six
Make direct amends to people whenever possible, except when to do so would injure them or others.

Step Seven
Continue to take a personal inventory of whether or not you are angry and when you are, promptly admit it.

The Twelve Suggested Steps

Excerpted from the Big Book of Alcoholics Anonymous

1. We admitted we were powerless over alcohol — that our lives had become unmanageable.

2. Came to believe that a Power greater than ourselves could restore us to sanity.

3. Made a decision to turn our will and our lives over to the care of God, *as we understood Him.*

4. Made a searching and fearless moral inventory of ourselves.

5. Admitted to God, to ourselves, and to another human being the exact nature of our wrongs.

6. Were entirely ready to have God remove all these defects of character.

7. Humbly asked Him to remove our shortcomings.

8. Made a list of all persons we had harmed, and became willing to make amends to them all.

9. Made direct amends to such people wherever possible, except when to do so would injure them or others.

10. Continued to take personal inventory and when we were wrong promptly admitted it.

11. Sought through prayer and meditation to improve our conscious contact with God *as we understood Him,* praying only for knowledge of His will for us and the power to carry that out.

12. Having had a spiritual awakening as the result of these steps, we tried to carry this message to alcoholics, and to practice these principles in all our affairs.

Affective Strategies

Overview of
Affective Strategies

Angry people usually have difficulty identifying other feelings. Anger is their mask and it has become the defense against a whole range of other feelings. Anger is a safety zone when other feelings create a sense of vulnerability that is difficult to tolerate. All feelings offer a gift; anger can energize, loneliness can lead to connection, guilt can make one more accountable, fear can offer protection. This section will assist clients in identifying and tolerating uncomfortable feelings. Learning to identify and tolerate feelings without the need to avoid or medicate them is an important goal in recovery. A strong aid to this section would be the use of Claudia Black's **Stamp Game**.

Feelings is a warm-up dialogue about feelings. In a brief and structured dialogue both facilitator and clients gain valuable information about the client's fears of showing a vulnerable self, and how they mask their vulnerability.

Hidden Feelings allows clients to consider the range of other feelings their anger could be masking prior to exploring other feelings specifically.

Experience of Fear begins the process of helping clients to recognize the fear that lies beneath much of their angry behavior. This session challenges them to look at what shaped their need to mask their fears; identify the beliefs of what would happen if they owned their fears; and to be more tolerant and accepting of their humanness as a person with fears.

Experience of Sadness begins the process of helping clients to recognize the sadness that lies beneath much of their angry behavior. This session challenges them to look at what shaped their need to mask their sadness; identify the beliefs of what would happen if they owned their sadness; and to be more tolerant and accepting of their humanness as a person with sadness.

Experience of Guilt acknowledges the client's relationship with guilt. The unhealthy expression of anger leaves them feeling guilty, yet many of them may not be conscious of the guilt. This session helps clients to own their guilt, distinguish the difference between true and false guilt, and develop tools to respond to those experiences for which they are guilty. The Shame sessions in the Cognitive Strategies section are strong complements to addressing guilt.

Experience of Pleasurable Feelings assists clients in understanding how it is they have great difficulty acknowledging and holding on to pleasurable feelings. This is an opportunity for them to begin to focus on the more positive aspects in their lives. The Words session in the Behavioral Strategies section is a good complement to this session.

Resentments acknowledges low level, slow burning anger and offers clients the opportunity to identify and let go of this festering and hurtful feeling.

Picture of the Unspoken is an art exercise that offers a different medium for identifying feelings of vulnerability other than anger. Making a collage is a valuable exercise for clients who are well defended through verbal skills or have difficulty saying anything — which describes most angry people. Engaging in an experiential form of therapy lessens defenses and offers containment allowing clients the safety to share more intimately about themselves.

Letting Go of Defensive Anger is a powerful exercise acknowledging how anger has influenced clients' lives, reinforcing how it has been a destructive defense, and facilitating a letting go process.

Forgiveness will give clients the opportunity to accept that even though their behavior has been hurtful to themselves and others, they are still worthy of self-forgiveness. While forgiveness is not a feeling, it can be both a behavioral and spiritual act, and it is an act of loving one's self.

Feelings

Objectives

To recognize behavioral masks that cover vulnerable feelings.
To identify fears related to expressing vulnerable feelings.

Materials Needed

Handout – Defenses As A Mask
Board

Starting Point

When people are frightened of their feelings, it is most likely they will find ways to defend against them. In this session clients begin the process of discussing feelings, owning difficult feelings, how they mask them and what they fear about their feelings. Begin by discussing the four questions in the handout Defenses As a Mask.

In the handout the first two questions prompt clients to begin talking about feelings; the third question helps them to identify how they mask feelings. Many times it is easier to recognize the behavior used to mask the feeling than to recognize the feeling. This can be a useful tool to help them pay attention to the behavior and use the behavior as a cue to identify feelings. The fourth question offers the opportunity to honestly acknowledge their fears. This is the beginning of putting their fears into a realistic perspective.

Ask your client to complete the handout, or if this is a group, ask them to share in dyads (groups of two). If you are working in dyads, once they are paired, ask them to respond to the first question and give them one minute for both people to respond. Then ask them to respond to the second question, allowing another minute. Question three needs you to give examples — allow them 2 - 3 minutes. When they address the fourth question allow as much time as they need.

Tell clients not to screen or filter their responses, just respond.

Share that feelings are a natural human experience. They are cues and indicators for what you need. Make the distinction that it is the distrustful expression of feelings that leads to difficulty, not the experience of feeling. Feelings can be used to help establish boundaries, to offer direction. Yet for most of us that is not what was learned.

Ask clients what messages they heard while growing up about feelings in general, and then specific feelings.

Discuss the messages they received, both verbal and nonverbal, that reinforced not showing feelings during their growing-up years. Put them on the board. You may receive examples such as:

If you show sadness you are weak, you are a sissy.
If you raise your voice you are out of control.
You have nothing to be angry about, and in fact you should be grateful.
That didn't really hurt.
If you don't stop your crying I will give you something to really cry about.

Discuss these examples. Then make the connection about how that makes it difficult to trust others. Remind clients that *recovery is learning to tolerate a range of feelings without the need to medicate, self destruct, or hide in anger.*

Defenses As a Mask

When you are frightened of your feelings it is natural that you find ways to defend against the feelings. Ultimately this interferes with your ability to identify feelings. By knowing your defenses, you are often in a better position to identify the feelings when they occur.

1. What are the feelings that are the easiest for you to demonstrate in front of people?

    _____

    _____

    _____

2. What are the more difficult feelings for you to show people?

    _____

    _____

    _____

3. Take one of those difficult feelings. When you begin to experience it, what do you do to defend against it? Do you mask it with another feeling, e.g. cover anger with sadness? Isolate? Intellectualize? Eat? Use humor? Other?

    _____

    _____

    _____

By recognizing what you do to mask your feelings, you are in a better position to identify more hidden feelings. For instance, if you hear yourself intellectualizing, knowing that is a defense to mask fear, you can now ask whether or not you are afraid. If you acknowledge using sarcasm to mask anger, you can own the anger when you hear your own caustic remarks.

4. Using the feeling you just described that you mask, what is the fear that gets in the way of your showing that emotion? (Don't screen your thoughts. The fear may not be rational, that's okay. It is only in recognizing it you can then address the fear.)

    _____

    _____

    _____

Hidden Feelings

Objective

To identify feelings masked by anger.

Materials Needed

Handout – Hidden Feelings

Starting Point

Chronically angry individuals are oversensitive to their own anger cues and under-sensitive to all or many of their other feelings. Anger is the mask for other feelings. Clients need to notice their range of feelings. The handout Hidden Feelings is a means to identify underlying vulnerable feelings.

Ask clients —

If they weren't so angry, what else would they be feeling?
If they were free of their anger what would they be feeling?
When they were in a situation in which they were angry, what were additional feelings?

Hidden Feelings

If I weren't so angry, what else would I be feeling?

_____

_____

_____

If I were free of my anger what would I be feeling?

_____

_____

_____

When I was in a situation in which I was angry, what were my additional feelings?

_____

_____

_____

Continue to ask yourself these questions at any time you experience any form of anger.

Experience of Fear

Objectives

To recognize childhood influences on the expression of fear.
To identify behaviors and beliefs related to experiencing fear.

Materials Needed

Handout – Family Influences on Fear
Handout – Expressing Fear

Starting Point

Fear is an extremely difficult emotion to own for persons dealing with anger problems. It is likely they have spent years distancing themselves from any connection to it.

To ease acknowledging fear, begin with a discussion of their growing up years and how family members influenced their expression of fear. Use the handout Family Influences on Fear to initiate this discussion.

Clients may feel extremely vulnerable talking about something they have spent years running away from. In the process of this discussion ask how they feel and pace them accordingly.

Offer clients the Expressing Fear handout. Although it is likely to be completed with greater honesty if combined with the other handout, it is less likely to create feelings of vulnerability.

Ask clients to identify situations they are presently feeling fear about and discuss what they can do to take care of themselves in a healthy manner.

Options will vary given their circumstances. Sometimes it is best to —

1. Recognize the feeling, and own it to yourself
2. Recognize the feeling, and share it with someone else
3. Engage in a relaxation technique
4. Journal
5. Engage in spiritual practice, and this may be as simple as reminding self with the Serenity Prayer (See Section Six: Faith Inspirations Handout, page 221)
6. Acknowledge that feelings are not there to hurt you, but for you to know yourself, and recognize your needs

Family Influences on Fear

Chronically angry people were most likely raised in a hurtful family system that often created a vulnerable state for children of a young age. While frequently experienced, fear was often denied. These fears, recognized or not, are carried into adulthood. In time, the denial lessens and you become aware of a great deal of fear and are unable to identify it. This fear is often referred to as "unidentifiable" or "free-floating" fear. In some instances, this fear can become pervasive (ever-present) or may appear episodically (appearing quickly and powerfully, then leaving almost as mysteriously). This fear may be experienced as anxiousness.

These exercises will help you to understand your relationship with fear.

Make a list of six situations that took place for you in your growing up years that you remember as being fearful whether or not you expressed that fear:

1. _____

2. _____

3. _____

4. _____

5. _____

6. _____

Check the behaviors that describe what you did as a child when you felt afraid:

☐ Acted like I was not afraid

☐ Cried

☐ Got angry

☐ Hid (Where?)

☐ Told someone about my fear (name) _____

☐ Other (fill in) _____

Check the most appropriate answers:

When I was afraid, my mom:

☐ Never noticed

☐ Noticed, but ignored it

☐ Made me feel embarrassed or ashamed

☐ Made me feel better

☐ Other (fill in) _____

When I was afraid, my dad:

☐ Never noticed

☐ Noticed, but ignored it

☐ Made me feel embarrassed or ashamed

☐ Made me feel better

☐ Other (fill in) _____

If you had a brother, sister or other significant person in your life who responded to your fear (either negatively or positively), describe how they responded:

_____

_____

_____

_____

_____

_____

_____

Expressing Fear

To better understand how you experience or react to fear today, complete the following sentences:

When I am afraid, I _____

_____

When I am afraid, I _____

_____

When I am afraid, I _____

_____

If people knew I was afraid, _____

_____

If people knew I was afraid, _____

_____

If people knew I was afraid, _____

_____

I'm never afraid because_____

_____

I'm never afraid because_____

_____

I'm never afraid because_____

_____

Experience of Sadness

Objectives

To recognize childhood influences on the expression of sadness.
To identify behaviors and beliefs related to experiencing sadness.

Materials Needed

Handout – Family Influences on Sadness
Handout – Expressing Sadness with Tears

Starting Point

To feel or express sadness is very frightening for people with anger problems. They judge themselves harshly, perceive themselves as weak, and experience profound loneliness around this pain. As with fear, they have gone to great lengths in their life to disconnect from this feeling.

To ease into acknowledging sadness, begin with discussing clients' growing up years. They may more readily accept that a child would feel sadness. Use the handout Family Influences on Sadness to begin this discussion and then continue with the handout Expressing Sadness with Tears.

Ask clients to identify situations they are presently feeling sad about and discuss what they can do to take care of themselves in a healthy manner.

Options will vary given the circumstances. Sometimes it is best to —

1. Recognize the feeling, and own it to yourself

2. Recognize the feeling, and share it with someone else

3. Engage in a relaxation technique

4. Journal

5. Engage in spiritual practice. This may be as simple as reminding self with the Serenity Prayer (See Section Six: Faith Inspirations Handout, page 221)

6. Acknowledge that feelings are not there to hurt you, but for you to know yourself, and recognize your needs

Family Influences on Sadness

There is always a great deal of loss in a home where you do not get the hugs you need, don't get the praise you deserve, or don't get the consistent parenting that is provided in healthy families.

With loss there is sadness, and with sadness there is often tears. Feeling sad and crying is a natural part of being human. If you did not receive validation for your sadness — if you experienced negative responses when expressing sadness, you probably began to control your expression of such feelings and attempted to control those of people around you, too. You may find yourself without the ability to cry, or find that after years of seldom crying, you are frequently crying and are unable to identify the reasons why there seems to be an over-abundance of tears.

The next few exercises are designed to enable you to identify your sadness and to help you to better understand how you perceive crying.

Things that are said or events that occur often cause sadness, but for many people sadness is caused by what isn't said or what didn't occur. For some, sadness is felt for all of the times they had to move, or for a parent never attending school events, or for never being told that they were loved.

Complete the following sentence:
When I was a child or teenager, I can remember feeling sad about (whether or not anyone else knew that you were sad):

1. _____
   _____

2. _____
   _____

3. _____
   _____

4. _____
   _____

Check the behaviors that describe what you did as a child when you felt sad:

☐ Cried when I was alone

☐ Cried in front of others

☐ Went to bed

☐ Took a walk

☐ Told someone about my sadness (name) _____

☐ Other (fill in) _____

☐ Other (fill in) _____

Check the most appropriate answers:

When I felt sad, my mom:

- ☐ Never noticed
- ☐ Noticed, but ignored it
- ☐ Made me feel embarrassed or ashamed
- ☐ Made me feel better
- ☐ Other (fill in) _____

When I felt sad, my dad:

- ☐ Never noticed
- ☐ Noticed, but ignored it
- ☐ Made me feel embarrassed or ashamed
- ☐ Made me feel better
- ☐ Other (fill in) _____

If you had a brother, sister or other significant person in your life who responded to your sadness (either negatively or positively), describe how they responded:

_____

_____

_____

_____

_____

_____

_____

_____

Expressing Sadness with Tears

To better understand how you experience the expression of tears today, complete the following sentences:

When I cry, I _____

_____

When I cry, I _____

_____

When I cry, I _____

_____

When I cry, I _____

_____

If people see me cry, I would _____

_____

If people see me cry, I would _____

_____

If you were unable to complete the first lines of the previous exercise because you never cry, complete the following statements:

I never cry because_____

_____

I never cry because_____

_____

If I ever did cry,_____

_____

If I ever did cry,_____

_____

I might have felt better if I'd cried when _____

_____

I might have felt better if I'd cried when _____

_____

Experience of Guilt

Objectives

To recognize childhood influences on the expression of guilt.
To distinguish between true and false guilt.
To identify present-day guilt.

Materials Needed

Handout – Family Influences on Guilt
Handout – Guilt

Starting Point

Clients with anger problems have demonstrated inappropriate behavior for which they are guilty. To feel the guilt facilitates social conscience. Many clients may be defensive, self-righteous, not owning guilt; others may feel guilt, but without new skills, they re-engage in hurtful behaviors. Some clients may have moved from feeling guilt to feeling shame, believing they are bad or inadequate rather than recognizing that it is their behavior that is bad or hurtful.

Guilt is about behavior — "I did something wrong" or "I made a mistake." Shame is about self — "I am the mistake." It may be helpful to coordinate the Shame sessions in the Cognitive Section with this Guilt module.

The handouts Family Influences on Guilt and Guilt will be helpful to clients who are beginning the process of understanding why they may struggle with guilt, owning their guilt, and distinguishing the difference between true and false guilt.

Discuss situations about which they are presently feeling guilt and explore avenues so they can take responsibility for their behavior. While apologies may be a place to begin, behavioral change is the true amends. Clients need to let go of expectations of others. Help them to understand that making amends is about being accountable – not about making the other person feel better or influencing their actions.

Ask clients to list and prioritize to whom they are accountable. Help them to problem solve and identify specific behaviors related to each person and situation.

Examples:

Guilt   — for not providing financial support to my son

Action   — begin to send some money, even if small amounts, monthly

Guilt   — for yelling at the grocer

Action   — go back to the store and apologize or mail a note of apology

Guilt   — for lying to my partner

Action — stay in this anger program

Make this an ongoing list that clients can add to as they develop greater awareness in the process of treatment. It needs to be reviewed periodically with clients so they can share the accomplishment of amends behavior, and/or problem solve possible strategies.

Family Influences on Guilt

Guilt is a feeling of regret or remorse about something you have or have not done. It is a healthy emotion that facilitates social conscience. For many people, guilt becomes distorted, particularly if they were raised in a troubled family.

It is helpful to make the distinction between true and false guilt. False guilt is feeling you are responsible for other people's behaviors and actions, such as believing you are responsible for your father's drinking, your mother's depression, or your parents' divorce. True guilt is feeling regret or remorse in response to your own behavior, i.e. lying, not doing what you promised.

List four situations in your growing-up years where you experienced true guilt.

1. _____

   _____

2. _____

   _____

3. _____

   _____

4. _____

   _____

Check the most appropriate responses that describe what happened when you felt guilty:

When I felt guilty, my mom:

- ☐ Never knew
- ☐ Reinforced my guilt by blaming me for things I did not do
- ☐ Made me feel even more guilt
- ☐ Punished me even if I was not at fault
- ☐ Overreacted in a negative way to my behavior
- ☐ Other (fill in) _____

When I felt guilty, my dad:

- ☐ Never knew
- ☐ Reinforced my guilt by blaming me for things I did not do
- ☐ Made me feel even more guilt
- ☐ Punished me even if I was not at fault
- ☐ Overreacted in a negative way to my behavior
- ☐ Other (fill in) _____

If you have difficulty distinguishing true guilt from false guilt, the following exercise will be helpful.

False Guilt
Write "No!" in each blank beginning each statement and then continue by finishing the sentence.

1. _____, I was not responsible for _____

_____

when he/she _____

2. _____, I was not responsible for_____

_____

when he/she _____

3. _____, it wasn't my fault when _____

_____

4. _____, it wasn't my fault when _____

_____

5. _____, it wasn't my duty or obligation to _____

_____

6. _____, it wasn't my duty or obligation to _____

_____

7. _____, I was only partially responsible for _____

_____

8. _____, I was only partially responsible for _____

_____

Guilt

Identify experiences in your adult life for which you have had or are experiencing guilt. If it is difficult to get started, list the names of significant people in your life, then circle the names of those about whom you have feelings of guilt:

1. _____   5. _____

2. _____   6. _____

3. _____   7. _____

4. _____   8. _____

I feel guilt in regard to (name) _____ about _____

I feel guilt in regard to (name) _____ about _____

I feel guilt in regard to (name) _____ about _____

Repeat that sentence as many times as necessary.

Examples might be:

> "I feel guilt in regard to my children about not showing up at our scheduled time to meet."

> "I feel guilt in regard to my coworker about telling her she was stupid."

> "I feel guilt in regard to my dog for kicking him in my anger."

Experience of Pleasurable Feelings

Objectives

To recognize childhood influences on the expression of pleasurable feelings.
To recognize beliefs that sabotage holding on to pleasurable feelings.
To identify pleasurable feelings today.

Materials Needed

Handout – Family Influences on Pleasurable Feelings
Handout – Expressing Pleasurable Feelings
Handout – Pleasurable Feelings Today

Starting Point

The client with anger problems frequently has difficulty experiencing pleasurable feelings as he/she is quick to accept invitations to anger and hesitant to hold more pleasurable feelings. This module will help clients to understand the underpinning for this confusing dynamic and begins the process of identifying that which gives them pleasure.

Have clients complete each of the three handouts in this section and then discuss them. The Pleasurable Feelings Today handout could also be incorporated as part of a session and then given as a daily assignment to assist clients in holding on to those feelings.

Family Influences on Pleasurable Feelings

As important as it is to be better able to identify feelings that are painful, it is just as important to experience feelings of pleasure.

Check the behaviors that describe what you did as a child when you felt happy:

☐ Laughed out loud

☐ Sang

☐ Walked in the woods

☐ Spent time with someone

☐ Played with my dog

☐ Wrote poetry

☐ Other (fill in) _____

☐ Other (fill in) _____

When I felt this way, my mom:

☐ Never noticed

☐ Noticed, but ignored it

☐ Did something to lessen the feeling

☐ Shared, supported, or participated in the feeling

☐ Other (fill in) _____

When I felt this way, my dad:

☐ Never noticed

☐ Noticed, but ignored it

☐ Did something to lessen the feeling

☐ Shared, supported, or participated in the feeling

☐ Other (fill in) _____

If you have a brother, sister, or other significant person in your life who responded to this feeling (either negatively or positively), describe how they responded:

_____

_____

_____

_____

_____

_____

_____

_____

Make a list of words that convey positive, warm feelings.

_____

_____

_____

Now complete the following sentence:

When I was a child or teenager, I can remember feeling *excited, happy, anticipation, giddy, love towards, loved* (insert your words) when:

1. _____

2. _____

3. _____

4. _____

Expressing Pleasurable Feelings

To better understand your resistance to showing positive feelings, complete the following:

Today I don't let others know when I feel positive feelings because:

_____

_____

_____

_____

What are the beliefs you are operating under that get in the way of expressing these feelings? What is the price you are paying as a result?

_____

_____

_____

_____

_____

_____

_____

_____

_____

_____

_____

_____

_____

_____

Experience of Pleasurable Feelings

Pleasurable Feelings Today

Today I feel _____ *(fill in the blank)* when:

_____

_____

Today I feel _____ *(fill in the blank)* when:

_____

_____

Today I feel _____ *(fill in the blank)* when:

_____

_____

Today I feel _____ *(fill in the blank)* when:

_____

_____

Today I feel _____ *(fill in the blank)* when:

_____

_____

Resentments

Objective

To explore the issue of resentments.

Materials Needed

Handout – Resentments
Board

Starting Point

Resentments are like burrs in a saddle blanket: if you do not get rid of them they fester into an infection. Resentments often stem from unrealistic expectations or distorted thinking and are experienced when someone is feeling discounted, slighted, or unheard. Ask clients to show with hands how many of them identify with carrying resentments. Ask them to identify the resentments they are carrying. List those on the board. If they have difficulty identifying resentments, use the following sentence stems to become focused.

I resent…
I resent it when…
I am resentful that…

Examples might be:
I resent that I have to be in this group.
I resent it when my wife tells me I remind her of her first husband.
I resent it when my son doesn't call me except when he needs money.
I am resentful that my co-worker was promoted and I wasn't.

Using one of the resentments from the board, explore ways to move from that place of resentment. One of the ways to move from resentment is to ask, what is the resentment covering? Is it covering up another feeling? Such as, resenting being in this group may more honestly be stated as, "I am afraid of some of my feelings that may surface in these sessions." "If I wasn't feeling resentful, I'd feel…" (afraid, sad, embarrassed, other)

Another way to move from resentment is to state what you need or what you would like. The resentment about being compared to a previous spouse could be stated as, "I need you to tell me what it is you are asking of me when you are upset." Resentment about always being called for money becomes, "I'd like you to call so we can talk, but don't ask for money again."

Appropriate statements would begin with:
I need …
I want …
I prefer …
I would like …

If a client's resentments are about feeling "less than," refer to the Shame Attacks session in Section Two.

Additional ways to move away from a place of resentment are:

1. If assuming, check the assumption
2. Put yourself in somebody else's shoes; it may allow your expectations to be more realistic
3. Be willing to live and let live

Give clients the Resentments handout and ask them to make a list of the little or big things they find themselves feeling resentment about on a daily basis until the next session. In the next session explore and discuss the lists they have made. Look for any themes regarding other feelings their resentments may be covering. Discuss their ability to state what they need or what they would like.

Resentments

On a daily basis, make a list of the little or big things you find yourself feeling resentful about.

Use the following sentence stems to garner clarity and direction for yourself.

1. I resent that …

    If I weren't feeling resentful, I'd feel …

2. I resent that …

    I need …

3. I resent that …

    I want …

4. I resent that …

    I prefer …

5. I resent that …

    I would like …

Picture of the Unspoken

Objective

To garner greater awareness of feelings.

Materials Needed

Collage materials for each client:
3 to 5 magazines (nearly any magazine can be used; it is suggested that there be an assortment)
14" x 17" pieces of paper, scotch tape, scissors

Starting Point

When situations and feelings are not acknowledged, not only are they discounted, the person experiencing them feels devalued. This is very destructive to a person's self-image. The willingness to acknowledge what has not been previously acknowledged is a step toward self-value. Have clients create a collage about the things they saw, heard or felt that caused them to feel devalued and which no one ever mentioned or did anything about.

A collage is made by taking pictures, words, and/or letters from magazines to make a statement. Depending on time, offer clients 20 to 30 minutes to create their collage. Suggest they begin their collage by flipping through a magazine and being open and receptive to what they see rather than looking for specific words or pictures. Part of the value in creating a collage is finding words or pictures that jump out at them and describe their feelings.

Share the following examples:

A picture of ...

1. an automobile may represent being with a parent when he/she was drinking and driving and never talking about it.
2. an attractive person may represent your own attractiveness that was never acknowledged by your parent.
3. a Christmas tree may represent a particular family fight that was never discussed.
4. a trophy may represent being selected for a school honor, yet your parents didn't attend the awards ceremony.

Additional collage work could focus on the exploration of specific feelings.

Examples:

Picture of fear — the fear may be from past and present experiences.

A picture of ...

1. a person of the opposite sex may represent that you are afraid of the opposite sex.
2. the word "no" may represent how difficult you find it to say no.
3. a hand may represent getting hit.

4. a cartoon showing a person walking on a tightrope may represent how fearful life is for you.

Picture of sadness — the sadness may be from past and present experiences.

A picture of ...

1. a smiling person may represent what you did to mask your sadness as a child.
2. the word "blue" may describe a color tone to your sadness.
3. a cloud may represent an intense amount of sadness and tears within you.
4. a woman may represent your mother, who reminds you of your greatest source of sadness.

Picture of guilt — the guilt may be from past and present experiences, false or true guilt.

A picture of ...

1. an obese person eating a multitude of sugars may represent what you do with guilt.
2. a child in leg braces may represent believing somehow you are responsible for injury in a car accident.
3. a bottle of liquor may represent guilt related to addiction.
4. a car racing down the road may represent symbolically speeding through life, trying to make up for your inadequacies, your guilt.

Picture of anger — the anger may be from past and present experiences.

A picture of ...

1. a volcano may represent how explosive and frightening you perceive your anger.
2. a bottle of alcohol may represent that you often drink to get rid of your anger.
3. a dog may represent being mad at your dad for giving your dog away when you were a kid.
4. a car may represent another form of escape when angry.

Picture of happiness — the happiness may be from past and present experiences.

A picture of ...

1. a forest may represent the feelings of peace and solitude you felt walking through the forest as a teenager.
2. a group of people all singing together may represent a feeling of belonging that you experience with certain friends (doesn't have to have anything to do with singing).
3. a family in a car may represent a positive family time.
4. books may represent when you are involved in learning something.

Remind clients that there is no right or wrong way to create a collage. Only they will interpret the pictures or words.

Letting Go of Defensive Anger

Objectives

To acknowledge how anger has influenced their lives.
To facilitate letting go of anger as a defense.

Materials Needed

Paper and pens

Starting Point

While anger is a natural human emotion, this session focuses on letting go of anger as a defense. Discuss the fact that it is only normal to develop defenses yet one must be cognizant of using them and recognize when they are more hurtful than helpful.

Didactic

Everyone develops defenses. Initially we create them to protect us from vulnerability and pain. They often become the mask for your fears and your shame. Unfortunately, you may continue to use those defenses in settings where protection is no longer needed and, in time, the defenses begin to interfere with your life. You don't want to give up the ability to protect yourself but you do want to choose healthier ways to do so.

Whereas anger is a feeling, for many it has become a defense, a blockade or barricade that interferes with the ability to connect with others in a healthy way. It ultimately interferes with the ability to get your needs met. The goal is not to ever be angry again, the goal is to quit using anger as a defense. Today you are going to do an exercise that is about letting go of anger employed as a defense.

As high a price as you may be paying for your anger, anger has at some point in your life been your friend, your companion. And anytime you lose a friend or something of value, you feel a loss. To cope with loss, it is helpful to create rituals of "letting go." To move forward you need to put the past behind you. In essence, it's important to say goodbye —goodbye to the rage, the rush, the intensity of anger, and the emotional addiction. So this exercise is about acknowledging the role anger plays in your life — the good and the bad — and then letting go of your attachment to anger as a solution to or defense.

Anger is not the only hurtful defense people use. Other hurtful defenses are denial, isolation, silence, intellectualizing, etc. But for the sake of this discussion, we are going to address anger. If you find this exercise helpful you can repeat it with other defenses that you recognize to be hurtful.

Ask clients to write a good-bye letter to their anger. The letter begins:

Dear Anger,

Thank anger for how it has served them. In essence, honor it. Then tell Anger how it is hurting them, causing them pain in their life; tell it that they need to let it go.

Read the following letter as an example:

Dear Anger,

I want to thank you for the help you have given me over the years. I needed you when I was just a kid. I never would have survived if I hadn't gotten tough and basically told the world to leave me alone. I was so scared and didn't want anyone to know. I was so ashamed of so much. I didn't want any one to see that shame. I couldn't let anyone get close to me. All they would have done is hurt me. You know, Anger, we had some good fights. Some of them made me feel so powerful, so strong, when I really felt weak and vulnerable. People were scared of me, and for a long time I liked that. But the truth is it's very lonely.
Because of you, Anger, I am in a lot of trouble. My kids are afraid of me like I was of my old man and mom. One of my kids doesn't even live at home. I can't keep a job. I work for myself because I can't get along with anyone else. To be honest, I am pretty miserable. My fear has never gone away, nor my shame, you have really just been a cover-up. It's odd, you once protected me from so much, my vulnerability, my shame, and now you are the source of my shame. I need to let you go.

Repeat the instructions:

1. Write Dear Anger.
2. Thank Anger for what it has done.
3. Tell Anger how it is now getting in the way.
4. Tell Anger that you now need to let it go.

Acknowledge that this may feel awkward but suggest they begin writing in spite of being uncomfortable.

Allow 10 - 20 minutes to write, then ask each client to read his or her letter out loud without stopping to explain, qualify, or defend — just read it slowly. When everyone has read their letter discuss what they learned about themselves and how they are feeling.

Often people can thank their anger and tell it how it has been causing pain in their life. When they do so, they are taking another step in letting go of this defense. Many times, though, they cannot honestly say they want to let it go, and in fact, could not write that. Ask them how many struggled with saying they're ready to let it go. Acknowledge how common that is, and then in discussion, address their ambivalence.

Clients who may be ambivalent should be asked relevant questions:

What part of Anger do they want to keep?

What purpose is it serving?

What do they need to be willing to let go of Anger as a defense (e.g. greater supports, better communication skills, apology, forgiveness, etc.)?

Whether or not they could sincerely say that they are ready to let their anger go, this exercise helps them to see anger as a defense, to acknowledge the negative consequences and to take responsibility for their willingness or unwillingness to let go.

Forgiveness

Objectives

To understand a framework for forgiveness.
To begin the process of self-forgiveness.

Starting Point

When someone begins to recognize how their behavior has been hurtful to others, they can quickly descend into a shame spiral. They think of themselves as bad and believe they are unworthy. This session helps clients begin to move out of their shame and into a place of greater self-esteem as a result of forgiving themselves.

Didactic

Recovery from the inappropriate expression of anger includes being accountable and responsible for how your anger has hurt others, and making amends if possible. But then you need to forgive yourself for having made mistakes, for being hurtful to others. While you may regret what happened, you can still forgive yourself. Forgiving means not holding on to the shame, which in the end is only more destructive.

Only in knowing what forgiveness means to you can you put it into a healing perspective.

Discuss what forgiveness means to the clients. What have they done that they would like forgiveness for? What would it mean to forgive oneself?

Discuss the reality that those whom they have wronged may not be ready or willing to forgive them. The wronged person may be unavailable or even deceased. But they can let go of their need to continue to judge and berate themselves.

In this discussion the following may be helpful:

By recognizing what forgiveness is not, it is more possible to see what forgiveness is.

What Forgiveness Is Not

Forgiveness is not forgetting.

Past experiences and the attendant pain have a great deal to teach you about not being victimized and about not victimizing others.

Forgiveness is not condoning.

You are not saying that what you did was unimportant, or "not so bad." It was important. It may have been hurtful.

Forgiveness is not absolution.

Forgiving does not absolve you from being accountable for your behavior. You are still responsible.

Forgiveness is not something that happens by making a one-time decision.

No matter how sincerely you want to let go of the past and move on with your life, you cannot just wave a magic wand and in one moment blithely make the past disappear. There is a process of grief work that you must walk through for forgiveness to occur.

What Forgiveness Is

Forgiveness is recognizing you no longer need your self-hatred, your self-pity.

You do not have to batter yourself. You are not destined to live a life of shame.

Forgiveness is no longer needing to punish yourself for your hurtful behaviors.

You hurt yourself in your behavior. Continuing to punish yourself no longer serves a useful purpose.

Forgiveness is an internal process; it happens within.

Forgiveness is remembering and letting go.

Forgive is something that occurs gradually over time.
As you do the work of healing, forgiveness will naturally begin to manifest itself in your life.

Self-forgiveness is difficult if a client is attached to shame-based beliefs, believing he or she should be punished, or is unclean or unworthy. When a client is resistant to self-forgiveness ask him or her, "What do you get out of maintaining the belief that you are not okay, or that you are bad?"

This is a discussion that very likely will be part of ongoing discussions.

Spiritual Strategies

Overview of
Spiritual Strategies

Spirituality is an aspect of life that is often ignored in therapy, yet it may be a crucial aspect of a client's recovery. People with anger issues are frequently angry with their God, feel abandoned and alienated from any Higher Power, or allow anger to be their Higher Source. For many, the spiritual disconnection fuels an internal dissension that keeps them in turmoil. Faith in the concept of a Higher Power or a loving spiritual power provides sustenance in the ongoing commitment to the healing process.

Sometimes clinicians experience more personal conflict in this area than those in treatment. Therefore it is important to address any personal biases and issues so that there is no interference with the potential that greater spiritual practice may offer your clients.

Spiritual History Discussion begins the process of talking about the client's experience with a spiritual connection.

Spirituality and Religious History assists the client in recognizing that one's childhood introduction to religion may influence their concept of spirituality.

Practicing Spirituality offers an opportunity to better understand the variety of spiritual practices and identify those that would be personally meaningful.

Faith Inspirations provides several popular passages that may be meaningful or inspirational in the practice of spirituality.

Spiritual History Discussion

Objective

To explore the role of a higher power and spiritual practices.

Materials Needed

Handout – Description of a Higher Power
Handout – Creating a Vision of a Higher Power

Starting Point

People who struggle with anger often have rigid or punitive beliefs about a higher power, or the role of God in their lives. Claims of being an atheist are frequently proferred as rigid defenses against trusting anything or anyone but themselves. Such strong beliefs may stem from believing that they have been abandoned by their God, or the need to be in control, or the consequence of religion having been used in a shaming manner.

Having faith in a loving power greater than oneself offers meaning in life and provides an inner calmness. This session explores the role of a higher power in one's life.

Begin by having clients complete the handout Description of a Higher Power. Then integrate the following discussion points.

Didactic

1. Give a short history of your religious involvement — whatever denomination, religious tradition or religious family experience from childhood until the present.

2. Who and what were the major influences on your religious and spiritual development as a child and adolescent, as an adult? (Significant persons, including parents — important books, institutions, situations, rites, events, etc. that influenced spiritually.)

3. Describe any unpleasant experiences or feelings related to religion or belief in God in your family or religious community. Be as specific as possible.

4. Describe any crisis points in spiritual development, other than those mentioned when answering question number three.

5. What is your present belief about God or a Higher Power in your life? Do you feel "connected" to God or a Higher Power? If so, what helps you to feel this way? Do you feel separated from God or a Higher Power? If so, what is causing this separation?

6. What is the most positive feature of your spiritual life at present?

7. Do you believe that spirituality, as you understand it, figures into your treatment or recovery journey? How?

8. What do you think would help you most to deepen and enhance you spiritual journey?

The handout Creating a Vision of a Higher Power is appropriate to pursue only if clients responded to question number seven affirmatively.

Description of a Higher Power

The following attributes will help you to clarify the image and experiences of your relationship with a Higher Power. Check the boxes that reflect or describe your relationship.

I experience a Higher Power as:

- ☐ Male
- ☐ Female
- ☐ An entity (God, Buddha, etc.)
- ☐ Existing within nature
- ☐ Other (describe) _____

I experience a Higher Power as:

☐ Loving	☐ Punishing	☐ Judgmental
☐ Distant	☐ Approachable	☐ Merciful
☐ Connected	☐ Angry	☐ Protective
☐ Fearful	☐ Ambivalent	☐ Faithful, loyal
☐ Shameful	☐ Sad	☐ Paternalistic
☐ Generous	☐ Kind	☐ Accepting

☐ Other _____

_____

_____

Creating a Vision of a Higher Power

Identify five qualities or characteristics you look for in a Higher Power.

1. _____

2. _____

3. _____

4. _____

5. _____

Write a want ad for the Higher Power you would like to have in your life.

_____

_____

_____

_____

_____

_____

_____

_____

_____

_____

_____

_____

Spirituality and Religious History

Objective

To explore how childhood introduction to religion may influence spirituality.

Materials Needed

Handout — Religious History

Starting Point

Religion and spirituality are not necessarily one and the same; therefore it may be helpful for clients to explore how their childhood experiences with religion may be influencing their concepts of spirituality. Give clients the handout Religious History.

Questions to explore are:

1. Were you forced to attend church or synagogue as a child, or otherwise participate in religious practices?

2. If your involvement in your church or synagogue ended, what made it stop?

3. If you didn't attend any type of church or religious service, how was that decision made?

4. If you were involved in a church or a religious group, describe your experience. Was it fun? Scary? Boring? Hopeful? Meaningful? Other?

5. Were there any particular rituals or ceremonies that you especially valued or that held significance for you? What were they?

Thoughts for Discussion or Didactic

- Unfortunately, many clients' experiences with religion have created inner conflicts for them that interfere with their openness to a spiritual path. All too often they feel very alone and confused, seemingly betrayed by the only Higher Power they have ever known. For many people, that Higher Power was steeped in the definition of a particular religion that was exclusive, rather than inclusive, which often led them to believe that their particular religion was the only way to have a meaningful relationship with a Higher Power. Based on that religion, people were taught The Golden Rule "Do unto others as you would have them do unto you." They were taught to be loving and honest and to respect their parents.

  In many families, however, children lived a contradiction between their religious teachings and what happened in their daily lives. Instead of respect, they were verbally abused. Instead of loving behavior, they witnessed one parent cause another intense anger or sadness. Instead of honesty, their parents lied, or they were told to lie for a family member under the guise of "protection." Did they get all dressed up, go to church, put on a smile, and then lie about why Mom or Dad was not there? How many times did they return home from church to neglect, abuse, or addiction kept hidden from the outside world?

- Most children truly believed in a Higher Power as it was portrayed in their house of worship but the contradiction of the religious messages within their family lives was too great for their continued commitment. Ask your clients:
  When you were growing up, how many times did you pray asking ...

  - for Dad to come home, but he didn't;

  - for Mom to be on time, but she was always late;

  - for Dad to stop hitting Mom, but he wouldn't;

  - for Dad to leave and never come back, but he stayed;

  - for Mom to protect you, but she didn't;

  - for Mom and Dad to be happy, but they never were;

  - for the abuse, the neglect, the illnesses, the hurts, and disappointments to be taken away, but they continued.

After being abandoned by their parents, thinking that God had not answered their prayers was, for many, the ultimate abandonment experience.

Spiritual pessimism and spiritual abuse are often created by religions that try to control by generating fear that one is innately evil or bad, and therefore may lose one's soul. Great numbers of unsuspecting trusting people have experienced spiritual abuse in the form of harmful beliefs couched in a religious framework. These are beliefs that fuel fear, unworthiness, guilt, and shame. If clients resonate with this experience, the didactic will enhance the discussion.

Didactic

In addition to contradiction between words and behavior, there are extreme situations of parents using their religious beliefs or practices as a way to directly, or indirectly, control their children.

Phyllis had to deal with the pain associated with her minister father always being away from home, attending to his "flock," while she and five other children were left home alone with their mother who was a raging alcoholic. When Phyllis was angry, periodically she yelled at her father in an effort to bring his attention to the pain going on at home and to the fact he was needed at home by his children. Not willing to hear his daughter's pleas for help, he would tell her to pray for forgiveness to the Almighty. Being angry was perceived as a sin. All painful feelings, particularly anger, were seen as being separate from God. To express that anger at an authority was a greater sin. To put your needs ahead of others (Dad's parishioners) was a higher sin.

In Phyllis' case, religious beliefs were used to induce guilt and shame, and in so doing, indirectly controlled her life.

Randy was forced to read the Old Testament repeatedly and then was quizzed by either his mother or his father before being able to spend time with friends. Randy was told it was the Bible that would dispense rewards. As a consequence, it was the Bible that was to become his punishing stick. In Randy's experience, the issue of control was very direct. These cases of abuse associated with religion are not necessarily actual religious practices advocated by a church's doctrine. These were abuses by very hurtful, frightened, shameful, controlling adults who used aspects of their religion to control and manipulate young children. Yet, when these same children become adults, it is often the religious doctrine they are angry with, not the people who framed it to suit their purpose. These dynamics within the family of origin often create extreme dislike, distrust, and ambivalence for anything related to the word "religion." Thus many clients spend much of their adult lives avoiding religion, while on a deeper level, searching for spiritual connection and fulfillment.

It is important to sort out "the messenger from the message" to develop a relationship with a doctrine whose tenets don't foster shame or mete out punishment. No one deserves to live in fear of a wrathful and punishing God. Everyone deserves to believe in the good of all, and that includes oneself.

Dialogue about whether or not your clients' religious beliefs were spiritually nourishing or spiritually abusive.

Religious History

It may be helpful to explore how your childhood experiences with religion may be influencing your concepts of spirituality.

Explore these questions:

1. Were you forced to attend church or synagogue as a child, or otherwise participate in religious practices?

   _____

   _____

2. If your involvement in your church or synagogue ended, what made it stop?

   _____

   _____

3. If you didn't attend any type of church or religious service, how was that decision made?

   _____

   _____

4. If you were involved in a church or a religious group, describe your experience. Was it fun? Scary? Boring? Hopeful? Meaningful? Other?

   _____

   _____

5. Were there any particular rituals or ceremonies that you especially valued or that held significance for you? What were they?

   _____

   _____

Practicing Spirituality

Objective

To introduce the concept of spiritual practice.

Materials Needed

Handout – Gratitude List

Starting Point

Spirituality is lived, practiced consistently, and acted on consciously. It is easy for people to discuss spirituality, but it is only experienced with practice.

Ask clients to describe their personal orientation toward spiritual practice by posing the following questions.

Are there spiritual practices you would like to explore? What are they?

What do you need to support these spiritual practices?

Are any of your behaviors or thoughts interfering with making a daily commitment to a spiritual life?

Didactic

To grow spiritually you must "walk the walk." Practicing spirituality means that you will:

- do the footwork;
- be present, be in the here and now;
- stay attuned to inner guidance;
- be authentic;
- let go of the attachment to results; and,
- believe in divine guidance and the choice it offers.

The practice of spirituality embraces gratitude as an attitude that brings a measure of happiness and a reminder to seek happiness. It is being grateful for what you have, instead of regretting what you do not have. In spiritual practice you learn tolerance and acceptance of both likenesses and difference, recognizing and understanding that all people struggle with fears and sorrows, and you do the best you can with what you have.

Ask clients to complete the handout Gratitude List, and suggest that they include this exercise as part of a daily ritual.

Practicing spirituality is taking time daily to honor the humanness of others and oneself, to appreciate the universe, and to give and share with others. Selfless service is a spiritual practice and it must be differentiated from the guilty need to rescue. Selfless service, or service from the self, is born of compassion and it is not performed out of its server's need, for in spiritual practice, what is offered to others is given freely and spontaneously. It comes from the heart, without expectation of return. In service, you experience the truth that "to give is to receive." Spirituality is the capacity to accept love, as well as the ability to give love. It is an instinctive empathy, an act of kindness, generosity, and intuitive thoughtfulness.

Your true self cannot be discovered from the outside. Your being can only be discovered in the silence of inner life. Your authentic identity reveals itself when the mind becomes quiet and you are fully conscious and present in the moment. The world is filled with noise and distractions from television to social chatter to unbidden thoughts. It is important to develop a process of turning off the external noise and tuning in the internal voice, the still quiet voice within.

There is no one right way to practice solitude. You might find that setting aside time at sunset to watch the changing colors, to feel the changing atmosphere, to hear the sounds at dusk and breathe in tune with the experience will take you right into that quiet place inside where you commune with that which is holy.

Spirituality is a process of going inward to the part of yourself that connects to the larger context. Some of the spiritual practices that connect you with your inner life are:

- prayer
- meditation
- the practice of silence/quietness
- guided imagery
- living a "thought"-full life

As you engage in spiritual practice, the location, the sounds, the time, and the use of materials often become significant and meaningful parts of your ritual. Many people include rituals involving deep breathing and relaxation. By definition, "spirituality" is derived from the Latin word spiritus, which means "the act of breathing." Breathing allows you to be open within your own body, to go "inside." Once your physical body is relaxed, it is easier to relax your mind and let go of thoughts and worries.

Prayer is common in church, ashram, or temple. It is also an important part of spiritual practice throughout the day. Some people have a favorite meditation book and include a reading from it during times of prayer. Some people get on their knees; others have a sitting area where they are surrounded by favorite objects, photographs, and plants. Prayer and/or meditation is something you can do while sitting in the living room, lying in bed, walking along the beach, or jogging in the park. Both prayer and meditation are practices that nurture and develop the connection to self and spirit. Prayer is an act that puts you in touch with a power greater than all else.

For many people, particularly those who have used keeping busy as a form of self-protection, the concept of meditation is particularly daunting. The idea of doing what appears to be "nothing", or "just being" is difficult to comprehend. Nevertheless, it is meditation that allows you to completely stop, to let go of thoughts about the immediate past or future, and simply focus on being in the here and now.

There are many books and classes on meditation. You may want to devise a source list for your clients.

Depending on the discussion, it may be appropriate to ask the clients what they would commit to do in exploring this aspect of their lives more fully.

Gratitude List

Today I am grateful for _____

_____

Today I am grateful for _____

_____

Today I am grateful for _____

_____

Today I am grateful for _____

_____

Today I am grateful for _____

_____

Faith Inspirations

Objective

To find meaning in spiritual messages.

Materials Needed

Handout – Desiderata
Handout – Faith Inspirations
Handout – Footprints
Handout – Praise to the Eternal Light
Handout – Native American Prayer

Starting Point

Spiritual messages and prayers have brought meaning to many. On the next several pages you will find a selection of handouts from which to choose. Share one or more of these selections with clients and discuss them.

What speaks to them in these messages?

When might this message have been heard and valued in their recent history?

Do they have a particular piece in which they find solace and meaning?

As an assignment, clients could be asked to bring a particular writing or an object that holds symbolic spiritual meaning for them.

Another assignment is to ask them to construct their own message or to paraphrase an existing message that has significant meaning for them and is one they would want to call upon to help them stay "present, in tune," or that lessens stress. Examples are, "Slow down, you're going too fast," "God be with me," "I am okay just as I am."

Faith Inspirations

Desiderata

(something desired as essential)

Go placidly amid the noise and the haste, and remember what peace there may be in silence. As far as possible, without surrender, be on good terms with all persons. Speak your truth quietly and clearly; and listen to the dull and ignorant; they too have their story. Avoid loud and aggressive persons; they are vexations to the spirit. If you compare yourself with others, you may become vain or bitter, for always there will be greater and lesser persons than yourself. Enjoy your achievements as well as your plans. Keep interested in your career, however humble; it is a real possession in the changing fortunes of time. Exercise caution in your business affairs for the world is full of trickery. But let this not blind you to what virtue there is; many persons strive for high ideals and everywhere life is full of heroism. Be yourself. Especially do not feign affection. Neither be cynical about love; for in the face of all aridity and disenchantment, it is as perennial as the grass. Take kindly the counsel of the years, gracefully surrendering the things of youth. Nurture strength of spirit to shield you in sudden misfortune. But do not distress yourself with imaginings. Many fears are born of fatigue and loneliness. Beyond a wholesome discipline be gentle to yourself. You are a child of the universe, no less than the trees and the stars and you have a right to be here.

And whether or not it is clear to you, no doubt the universe is unfolding as it should. Therefore, be at peace with God, whatever you conceive Him to be. And whatever your labors and aspirations, in the noisy confusion of life, keep peace with your soul.

With all its sham, drudgery and broken dreams, it is still a beautiful world. Be cheerful. Strive to be happy.

Max Ehrmann, 1927 ©Robert L. Bell

FAITH INSPIRATIONS HANDOUT

Faith Inspirations

God grant me the SERENITY to accept the things I cannot change
COURAGE to change the things I can, and WISDOM to know the difference.

Serenity Prayer, Reinhold Niebuhr, 1892-1971

Ah! Your very being is the perfect teacher.
Recognizing your nature, take this to heart.
For all those who have not realized this, arouse compassion,
To help them find this pure and holy space.

Buddhist Invocation

The seed of the Blessed One is planted in us, but we have trouble accepting this reality. Our deepest fear is not that we are inadequate. Our deepest fear is that we are powerful beyond measure. It is our light, not our darkness, that most frightens us. We ask ourselves, who am I to be brilliant, gorgeous, talented and fabulous? Actually, who are you not to be? You are a child of God.

Marianne Williamson

I am a stag of seven times.
I am a wild flood on the plain.
I am a wind on the deep waters.
I am a tear the sun lets fall.
I am a hawk above the cliff.
I am a salmon in the pool.
I am a battle-waging spear.
I am a wave of the sea.
Who but I knows the mystery of the unhewn man?

From The Song of Amergin, Celtic Traditional

Footprints

One night I dreamed a dream. I was walking along the beach with my Lord. Across the dark sky flashed scenes from my life. For each scene, I noticed two sets of footprints in the sand, one belonging to me and one to my Lord.

When the last scene of my life flashed before me, I looked back at the footprints in the sand and to my surprise I noticed that many times along the path of my life there was only one set of footprints. I realized that this was at the lowest and saddest times of my life.

This always bothered me and I questioned the Lord about my dilemma. "Lord, you told me when I decided to follow You, You would walk and talk with me all the way. But I'm aware that during the most troublesome times of my life there is only one set of footprints. I just don't understand why, when I needed You most, You leave me."

He whispered, "My precious child, I love you and I will never leave you, never, ever, during your trials and testing. When you saw only one set of footprints, it was then that I carried you."

©1964 Margaret Fishback Powers

Praise to the Eternal Light

Praise to the refuge of all.

Praise to the Most Merciful.

Praise to him who is eternal purity.

Praise to the spotless One.

Praise to the Destroyer of sin.

Praise to the Protector of the just.

Praise to the Remover of ignorance.

Praise to the divine Light.

Praise to the true Light.

Praise to the Light of life.

Praise to the Light of the world.

Praise to the Light of the self.

Praise to the inner Light.

Eternal Light, shining beyond the heavens, radiant Sun, illuminating all regions, above, below, and across, true Light enlightening every person coming into the world, dispel the darkness of our hearts and enlighten us with the splendor of your glory. Amen

Adapted from the Indian liturgy

Native American Prayer

Oh, Great Spirit, whose voice I hear in the winds,
and whose breath gives life to all the world, hear me.
I am small and weak. I need your strength and wisdom.

Let me walk in beauty and make my eyes ever behold
the red and purple sunset.

Make my hands respect the things you have made.
Make my ears sharp to hear your voice.
Make me wise so that I may understand
the things you have taught your people.

Let me learn the lessons you have hidden
in every leaf and rock.

I seek strength, not to be greater than my brother,
but to fight my greatest enemy — myself.

Make me always ready to come to you
with clean hands and straight eyes.

So when life fades, as the fading sunset,
my spirit may come to you without shame.

Closing Strategies

Overview of
Closing Strategies

It is very likely that people with anger issues have few or poor experiences with closure. The sessions offered here allow for a process of acknowledging a commitment the client has made to him/herself; acknowledging new skills; and are an opportunity for self-validation and affirmation.

Healing and Recovery Tools offers an opportunity to identify specific tools that the client acknowledges as helpful in sustaining their recovery and reinforces the use of these tools.

Moving on with New Skills reinforces newly learned skills and creates a basic relapse prevention plan.

Closing Ritual with affirmations is an effective closing for either a group or individual. If working with a group this can be a full session; with an individual, it can be the closing portion of their last session.

Healing and Recovery Tools

Objective

To identify and reinforce the use of available tools for recovery.

Materials Needed

Handout – Recovery Tools

Starting Point

To sustain a newly learned skill, it is important for clients to incorporate specific tools into their daily lives. Review the list on the Recovery Tools Handout and ask clients to add other known tools to the list. Tools need to be specific to the client. Have clients circle the recovery tools they already practice consistently and check those they would like to incorporate or practice more consistently.

Then, ask them to identify one to three recovery tools they will commit to using in the next day and/or week. Do not overwhelm them with expectations. Be realistic. Change occurs slowly. If clients could make changes readily, they would. Therefore, you will need to discuss in detail which tools they will use. Facilitator needs to use personal judgment as to the number of new tools appropriate to introduce. Problem solve their concerns, etc. Slowly build the use of more and more of these tools into their daily lives.

Have the clients complete the handout and then discuss it. This is a helpful exercise for them to complete as a form of self-monitoring and reporting to the clinician on a regular basis.

Recovery Tools

Circle the behavior(s) you practice consistently.
Check (✔) the behavior(s) you are willing to incorporate in to your daily life or practice more consistently.
Keep this handout with you and circle the day(s) of the week that you use each recovery tool.

		Sun	Mon	Tues	Wed	Thurs	Fri	Sat
☐	Practice positive thinking	Sun	Mon	Tues	Wed	Thurs	Fri	Sat
☐	Utilize affirmations	Sun	Mon	Tues	Wed	Thurs	Fri	Sat
☐	Utilize relaxation techniques	Sun	Mon	Tues	Wed	Thurs	Fri	Sat
☐	Practice counter-thoughts to negative thinking	Sun	Mon	Tues	Wed	Thurs	Fri	Sat
☐	Participate in physical activity	Sun	Mon	Tues	Wed	Thurs	Fri	Sat
☐	Take my medication (if applicable)	Sun	Mon	Tues	Wed	Thurs	Fri	Sat
☐	Pray, meditate, or call upon Higher Power	Sun	Mon	Tues	Wed	Thurs	Fri	Sat
☐	Write in journal	Sun	Mon	Tues	Wed	Thurs	Fri	Sat
☐	Share with another in my support system	Sun	Mon	Tues	Wed	Thurs	Fri	Sat
☐	Attend support group	Sun	Mon	Tues	Wed	Thurs	Fri	Sat
☐	Eat healthy	Sun	Mon	Tues	Wed	Thurs	Fri	Sat
☐	Participate in fun activity	Sun	Mon	Tues	Wed	Thurs	Fri	Sat
☐	Set appropriate limits/boundaries	Sun	Mon	Tues	Wed	Thurs	Fri	Sat
☐	Say Yes	Sun	Mon	Tues	Wed	Thurs	Fri	Sat
☐	Say No	Sun	Mon	Tues	Wed	Thurs	Fri	Sat

List other recovery tools specific to you.

1_____ Sun Mon Tues Wed Thurs Fri Sat

2_____ Sun Mon Tues Wed Thurs Fri Sat

3_____ Sun Mon Tues Wed Thurs Fri Sat

4_____ Sun Mon Tues Wed Thurs Fri Sat

5_____ Sun Mon Tues Wed Thurs Fri Sat

Moving On with New Skills

Objectives

To reinforce newly learned cognitive and behavioral skills.
To create an ongoing recovery plan.

Materials Needed

Handout – Moving On with New Skills

Starting Point

This session offers clients the opportunity to reflect on what they have learned and it can be a relapse prevention plan. It will reinforce newly acquired skills, identify relapse triggers with a plan of action, and identify a support base.

It is suggested the handout Moving On with New Skills be offered as a focus for discussion to facilitate greater opportunity for clients to be more specific.

Moving On with New Skills

What have you learned about yourself and your anger that is helpful?

1. _____
2. _____
3. _____
4. _____

What constructive behaviors are you incorporating into your daily life?

1. _____
2. _____
3. _____
4. _____

What are your self-defeating attitudes and behaviors that you need to pay attention to?

1. _____
2. _____
3. _____
4. _____

When you observe these behaviors and attitudes, what are you willing to do?

1. _____
2. _____
3. _____
4. _____

Who is your support system?

1. _____
2. _____
3. _____
4. _____

Closing Ritual

Objective

To experience a healthy closure in treatment.

Materials Needed

Optional: Certificate, coin, or another token of treatment completion

Starting Point

People with anger problems often have difficulty receiving validation and they also have difficulty with healthy closure. This session provides suggestions for validation and closure whether the facilitator is working with a group or an individual.

Closing ritual:

- As each client in the group takes a turn, the others one by one, share with them an affirmation.
  Examples are:
    What I really value about you is —
    What I have most appreciated about you is —

- Present a tangible object such as a certificate, coin, or another symbol of their completion and moving on as an affirmation of the clients' commitment to their recovery process.

- Offer an imagery of affirmation and closure to the clients' experiences in these sessions.

Imagery Direction

This closing imagery is **not** on the **Imageries** CD. You are welcome to create your own version of the scripted imagery. The key is to talk slowly and allow the clients time to breathe deeply, to hear the words, to "be" with the words. Playing soft music as a background to accompany the imagery is pleasing.

Begin the experience by asking clients to find a comfortable sitting position, uncross their arms and legs, and begin to take slow deep breaths in and out. As you offer these directions, pace your speaking so that it is soothing and relaxing.

Closure Imagery

Slowly breathe in… and out.

Breathe in… and out.

As you breathe in, imagine healing energy beginning to move throughout your body. Allow the muscles in your face, neck and shoulders to soften and relax. Breathe in calming energy… breathe out tension. Feel this calm and healing energy move down through your chest and arms into your waist and legs. Feel your stress and tension melt away. Feel your connection to your Higher Power. Know that you are safe in this room and you are loved.

Begin to visualize all of the tools you have gathered to strengthen your recovery. You have tools to focus on relationships, powerlessness, control, shame, secrets, anger, feelings, and many other aspects of your life which are important in recovery.

Today, you will focus on many of these tools and remember that you have done a great deal of work to strengthen your recovery and prevent relapse. You are never immune to relapse, but if you choose to use your tools each day, your recovery is strengthened.

You have tools to help you focus on healthy, nurturing relationships.

Say to yourself —
> **I deserve to have a healthy and nurturing relationship with myself.**

You have tools for letting go of control.

Say to yourself —
> **Today, I choose to let go of my resentments and control.**
> **Today, acceptance is the answer to all my problems.**
> **Today, I will let my Higher Power guide my journey.**

You have tools for releasing shame and secrets.

Say to yourself —
> **Today, I choose to release shame messages I have received from others and shame I have about myself.**
> **I choose to surround myself with healthy people in my recovery.**
> **Today, I choose to live my life in honesty and recovery.**

You have tools for releasing anger.

Say to yourself —
> **Today, I choose to release my anger.**
> **I choose to live my life filled with serenity and peace.**
> **I choose to surround myself with people who are serene and peaceful.**

You have tools for your grief and other feelings.

Say to yourself —

Today, I know that I am safe to have feelings and I can choose to express my feelings.

Today, I choose to surround myself with people who are safe to express my feelings with.

You have tools for when you may experience warning signs and triggers.

Say to yourself —

I may experience warning signs and triggers.

If I do, I will immediately use my relapse plan and ask others for help.

I am not alone in my recovery.

People who love me and support my recovery surround me in my recovery program.

I am not alone.

Today, my program of recovery is the most important thing in my life.

If I make anything or anyone else more important than my program, I may have a relapse.

Today, I have the tools to nourish my spiritual program of recovery.

Remember, these tools work only when you use them. Each day in recovery, it is important to use these tools wisely.

Say to yourself —

I am precious.

I am worthy of recovery.

I love myself.

I am able to receive love and support from others.

As you continue to breathe deeply, slowly and gently become aware of your body in this room. Become aware of your head... your neck... your shoulders and arms. Become aware of your back... your chest... your waist... your legs... your feet. Become aware of your connection to the earth. Gently begin to shift your body around and when you are ready, open your eyes.

Closing Thoughts

Dear Facilitator,

Working with people with anger problems is undoubtedly complex and challenging. At the same time it can be equally rewarding. My experience tells me that these are shame-based people who found anger to be a solution to their pain, and gave them what they could not learn more naturally.

It is my hope that Anger Strategies will empower them to share their vulnerability, adopt more constructive belief systems, and develop skills that build their self-esteem and lead to healthier behaviors. Thank you for being a part of this process.

Resources by Claudia Black, Ph.D.

Strategies Series:
Anger
Depression
Family
Relapse

Books
A Hole in the Sidewalk
Changing Course
It Will Never Happen To Me
It's Never Too Late To Have A Happy Childhood
My Dad Loves Me, My Dad Has A Disease
Repeat After Me
Straight Talk

Videos
Anger
Addiction in the Family
The Baggage Cart
Breaking the Silence
Healing from Childhood Sexual Abuse
The History of Addiction
Issues of Recovery
The Legacy of Addiction
Process of Recovery
Relapse: Illusion of Immunity
Relationship Series
Roles
Shame
What Do I Say To My Kids?

CDs
A Time for Healing
Imageries
Letting Go Imageries
Putting the Past Behind

Games
The Stamp Game: A Game of Feelings

To order materials or arrange a speaking engagement with
Claudia Black, Ph.D., contact

Claudja Inc. dba MAC Publishing
#346 • 321 High School Rd NE Ste D3
Bainbridge Island WA 98110-2648
206.842.6303 Voice • 206.842.6235 Fax
www.claudiablack.com